Eyewitness
ECONOMY

Native-American shaman's rattle from the Pacific Northwest

A shekel of pearl barley

Diamonds

大明通行寶鈔

壹貫

Emblem of the Society of Pewterers, New York City

SOLID AND PURE

Paper currency from 14th-century China

Basket of household goods

DEBIT CARD
4539
4444 8888 5555 0000
MONTH/YEAR
05/06 EXPIRES 06/09
VALID FROM
NR
END

DEBIT CARD
5555 0000
MONTH/YEAR
05/06 EXPIRES 05/09
VALID FROM
NR
END

Debit cards

Multicolored
beads used as currency

Eyewitness
ECONOMY

80 Indian rupees
and one British pound

Written by
JOHNNY ACTON
and
DAVID GOLDBLATT

Bull and bear ornaments

Ears of wheat

The Medici family coat of arms

Apple iPod

DK

LONDON, NEW YORK, MELBOURNE, MUNICH, AND DELHI

Consultant Professor Sean Masaki Flynn
Scripps College, California

Senior editor Rob Houston
Editorial assistant Jessamy Wood
Managing editors Julie Ferris, Jane Yorke
Managing art editor Owen Peyton Jones
Art director Martin Wilson
Associate publisher Andrew Macintyre
Reference section Q2AMedia
Picture researcher Louise Thomas
Production editor Melissa Latorre
Production controller Charlotte Oliver
Jacket designer Johanna Woolhead
Jacket editor Adam Powley
US editor Margaret Parrish

DK DELHI

Editors Alka Ranjan, Ankush Saikia
Designers Mitun Banerjee, Govind Mittal
DTP designers Dheeraj Arora, Preetam Singh
Project editor Suchismita Banerjee
Design manager Romi Chakraborty
Production manager Pankaj Sharma
Head of publishing Aparna Sharma

Nuts and berries

Russian nesting dolls

First published in the United States in 2010 by
DK Publishing, 375 Hudson Street, New York, New York 10014
Copyright © 2010 Dorling Kindersley Limited
10 11 12 13 14 10 9 8 7 6 5 4 3 2 1
175397—12/09
170-3218

A catalog record for this book is available from the Library of Congress.

ISBN: 978-0-7566-5826-7 (Hardcover)
978-0-7566-5827-4 (Library Binding)
Color reproduction by MDP, UK, and Colourscan, Singapore
Printed and bound by Toppan Printing Co. (Shenzhen) Ltd., China

Discover more at
www.dk.com

Fruits on display

Gas pump nozzle

Contents

Chinese coins

What is the economy?

ALL ABOUT MONEY?
You might think that the economy is only about money, but money is just a temporary, symbolic store of wealth. It is not useful in itself—its value lies solely in the fact that it can be exchanged for things that people need or want.

IMAGINE THAT YOU HAVE A THOUSAND dollars to live on for a month. With this money, you have to stock up on food, pay rent and utility bills, buy a new pair of shoes, and get your computer repaired. Too many needs and too little money? Well, that is what the economy is all about—using limited resources to fulfill a great many needs. The word economy comes from a Greek word meaning "one who manages a household," but when people use the term they are usually referring to their home nation or to the world as a whole. The economy of a region is determined by the choices its people make about what to produce, what to buy, and what to spend, given the limited resources. Economics is the study of how people make these choices and the consequences of their decisions.

WHERE DO I FIT IN?
Everybody is part of the economy. Whenever you buy, sell, or exchange something, you are also contributing to the economy in a small way. Every single music download contributes to a global multi-billion-dollar music industry.

Tally of livestock

KEEPING ACCOUNT
This 5,500-year-old clay tablet from ancient Mesopotamia contains a record of a tally of sheep and goats. The Mesopotamians were the first people to develop a system in which goods produced, traded, and stored were recorded. To do this effectively, they invented writing.

Container ship in Istanbul port, Turkey

MANUFACTURING

The manufacture of goods is a major part of the economy today. It makes up around one-third of the total value of global economic activity. In many industries, the process of manufacturing is split into specialized tasks that require specific skills. This auto factory worker specializes in making a single part of an engine.

AGRICULTURE

Once the most important sector in almost all economies, agriculture now accounts for just 4 percent of the world's economic output. It is still the largest sector in some countries, however. In the Republic of Guinea-Bissau, western Africa, cashew nuts are the major source of the nation's income.

Cashew nut _____

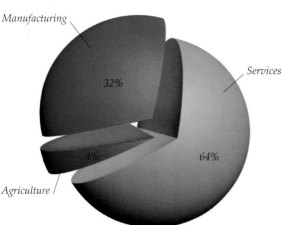

Manufacturing

Services

32%

4%

64%

Agriculture

SECTORS OF THE ECONOMY

Economies can be divided into three main sectors: agriculture, manufacturing, and services. Their relative importance can vary greatly between nations, but, in general, as a country develops (gets richer), the importance of agriculture decreases and the services sector becomes larger. This pie chart shows the contributions of each of the three sectors to the world economy.

Guide showing tourists the sights in Egypt

SERVICES

The economy is not just about making things. Services are an important part of it, too. Service industries include banking, health care, education, and tourism. A tourist guide does not offer a physical product. Instead, people pay him to show them around an attraction because he knows the place well. Service industries form the largest sector of the global economy.

GLOBAL TRADE

Modern methods of transportation and communication have created a truly global economy. People send vast quantities of goods around the world as they trade with one another. Some goods, such as coal and oil, travel in bulk, but most go in containers. Trade is now so interconnected that across the world, a single standard-size container transports 90 percent of all nonbulk cargo—in ships, trains, and trucks.

Standard-size container

Crane loading containers

Economic goals

INDIVIDUALS MAKE PERSONAL CHOICES such as what job to accept or how much to spend on a new car, whereas governments make collective decisions that affect the whole society, such as whether to tax the rich more than the poor, and how much to spend on roads and bridges. Some economic decisions affect the welfare of the entire planet, while others have a more local focus. For some governments, the wealth of the nation as a whole is what matters. For others, it is more important that wealth is divided as equally as possible among the people. Some governments aim to provide free basic facilities to all their citizens. All governments, however, need to consider short- and long-term gains before they make economic decisions.

A PICTURE OF WEALTH
The luxurious Burj Al Arab hotel in Dubai in the United Arab Emirates (UAE) was developed by, and caters to, the super rich. In the UAE, the richest 0.2 percent of the population controls 90 percent of the wealth. So while business people pursue their personal goals of immense private wealth, there is little benefit for the society as a whole.

CHOICES AND PRIORITIES
People make economic choices due not only to their preferences, but also to their circumstances, such as whether they are healthy or they have a family to support. Their choices also depend on what is happening in the wider economy. These people are living in unstable times in Iraq and cannot make long-term plans. They need to hear the news, which could be why they have invested in satellite TV, even though their house is badly in need of repair.

A PRICE TO PAY
Being rich is attractive to individuals, but people may have to work long hours and have minimal contact with their families to achieve this goal. Whether people are prepared to do this depends on whether they feel the sacrifices are worth it.

EQUAL EARNERS

In Sweden, the difference in income between the highest and lowest earners is much smaller than in other countries because the government taxes the rich more than the poor. This system allows the citizens to enjoy a good quality of life and makes them feel they are all in it together. Not everyone is happy, though. Some Swedes resent paying high taxes so that the government can provide support to people in need.

HEALTH CARE FOR ALL

Governments differ in the focus of their economic policies. Some countries, such as Brazil, Britain, Canada, and Japan, provide free health care to all their citizens. The governments raise the money for these services through taxes. In other countries, people need to organize their own private insurance plans to fund their health care.

AN EQUAL WORLD

Some governments organize their economies to minimize the differences in wealth between their citizens. In China, at one time people were even required to wear identical clothes. A major drawback of this system is that it takes away one of the biggest incentives for people to come up with new ideas—the chance to get rich. Another problem is that those with power may be tempted to pay themselves more than the rest. However, the advantage of such a system is that housing, education, and medical facilities are provided to all citizens.

TOO MUCH TOO SOON

Economic goals may focus on short-term gains without considering the future. Residents of the Pacific island of Nauru grew rich relatively quickly by mining the phosphates that were the tiny nation's major natural resource, but they had to pay a high price in the long term. With the phosphate now exhausted, there is only about one acre (half a hectare) of agricultural land left, and all the island's food has to be imported. Some see this as a warning about what could happen to the entire planet if people are not careful with Earth's natural resources.

Who decides?

THE WAY AN ECONOMY FUNCTIONS depends on who is making decisions about it. In one economic system, known as a command economy, everything—from what goods and services to produce, to how to distribute them—is planned by the government. In another, called the free market system, there is no central authority calling the shots. Instead, decisions are made by individual people and businesses. This can work well all by itself, but free markets can face problems when there are too few buyers or sellers. If just one company sold an essential item such as water, for instance, it could charge very high prices, and if there were very few buyers for bananas, the sellers would be forced to reduce their prices to ridiculously low levels. As a result, most nations have a mixed economy in which businesses run their own affairs, but their activities are regulated by the government.

Carpet displayed to attract customers

THE INVISIBLE HAND
Adam Smith believed that the free market economy was guided by an "invisible hand" that matched up people's wants and needs to everyone's advantage. No one forces these carpet sellers to group together, but because they do, customers know exactly where to go to buy carpets. Customers also benefit from low prices as sellers compete for their money. Meanwhile, the sellers are guaranteed plenty of customers. Everybody wins, but no one planned the system in advance.

Communist Party headquarters, Beijing, China

COMMAND ECONOMY
A communist economy is a type of command economy. Communism is a political and economic philosophy that favors a classless society where there are no rich or poor people, and everyone is equal. In a communist country the state owns all the means of production such as factories, tools, and raw materials, and decides what the needs and wants of the people are. China's communist goverment decides in advance much of what its people are going to grow and manufacture.

PEOPLE'S CHOICE
In democratic nations, governments are chosen by voters. Political candidates present their economic policies (plans), and voters decide whom to elect. People have the power to vote the government out of office if they do not think it is doing a good job of managing the nation's economy. This woman is voting for her preferred candidate in Indonesia's 2009 elections.

Ballot paper marked to indicate voter's choice

TOTAL CONTROL
In a dictatorship, one person has complete control over all economic activities (and almost everything else). This benefits the dictator, but the people have little choice. President Saparmurat Niyazov of Turkmenistan made sure that much of his nation's oil and gas wealth went to himself. He used some of this money to commission a solid gold statue of himself that rotated to follow the Sun.

WHERE THE CONSUMER IS KING
In free market or mixed economies, consumers are free to spend their money on whatever they choose. Their choices determine what is produced in the economy. If people are willing and able to pay for a certain product, there is an incentive for someone to produce it. Often, many companies compete—making the same product and giving consumers a range of brands to choose from.

BANANA REPUBLICS
Sometimes businesses are so large and powerful, they control the economy of a region. The US-owned United Fruit Company once dominated the economy of Central America to such an extent that the countries in this region became known as "banana republics."

Making choices

PEOPLE EVERYWHERE FACE economic decisions. They must decide how to make the best use of their limited resources. This is true now and was just as true thousands of years ago, before agriculture was invented. At that time, everyone lived by hunting and gathering their own food, moving from place to place, and by making tools and shelters out of local materials. They lived in small, mobile groups, and might have traded occasionally with other groups. Economists say they had a hunter-gatherer economy. Some people still live as hunter-gatherers today. There are others who make a living by small-scale farming, or by grazing animals. Their economies are small in scale, but they face the same economic decisions as people in industrialized societies, such as how to cooperate and divide their labor and how to care for the young and the sick.

Fish

Eggs

Nuts

Berries

UNCHANGED LIVING
A few hunter-gatherer communities that remain today continue to live in a way that has changed little for thousands of years—hunting and gathering food rather than farming it. Men usually fish and hunt animals, and women gather nuts, eggs, and berries. Surviving hunter-gatherer societies provide us with important clues about how our ancestors lived in the distant past.

Bushmen take aim, while hiding in long grass

Bow

Arrow

HUNTING TOGETHER
These Bushmen from the Kalahari Desert in Namibia, Africa, work together because they know that they are much more likely to make a kill if they cooperate than if they hunt separately. If the hunt is successful, the meat will be shared by all, because sharing is vital in such societies. There are rarely stores of surplus food, so everybody must eat when food is available.

SPECIALIZATION
A universal feature of all human economies is specialization, or division of labor. This is evident in small-scale societies such as the Yanomami tribe of the Amazon rain forest in South America. No Yanomami man would dream of chewing cassava root, which the women of the tribe do ahead of cooking to remove its bitterness. The whole community, however, benefits from the results of the labor.

Yanomami woman preparing cassava in the Amazon rain forest

NOMADIC LIFE
Pastoralists are people who keep animals but move continually with them in search of fresh pasture. They lead a nomadic life, moving from place to place. They set up temporary homes where they expect to find resources such as food, water, and material for tools. These Mongolian herders live in portable felt tents called yurts or gers.

Strips of metal make a rattling sound

HEALING POWERS
Small hunter-gatherer communities have their own methods of dealing with sickness and disease. Some people in these communities specialize in the healing properties of the plants in their area. They are believed to have spiritual powers and perform rituals to deal with spirits that they believe cause disease. In some communities, spiritual leaders called shamans use rattles to conduct healing ceremonies.

Shaman's rattle, Pacific Northwest, US

UPHOLDING TRADITION
Hunter-gatherer communities are fast disappearing as their members rush to join the global economy. But some communities, such as the Pila Nguru Aboriginals of Western Australia, have chosen to maintain their traditional lifestyle, including producing colorful dot paintings, despite contact with industrialized societies.

Owning things

Most people take it for granted that certain things belong to them—typically gifts, or things they have made themselves or have worked to get. People have rights over the things they own, but these are different in every society. A hunter-gatherer would find the idea of a person owning land very strange, and in communist countries, factories and raw materials are owned by everyone, but in effect, by the state. In ancient Rome, people could own other people (slaves), and until the late 19th century, married women in many European countries had no legal property rights. Ownership affects people's economic choices, since it determines the return they get from their hard work or investment. So property rights are central to how an economy works.

ALL MINE!
Chimpanzees seem to have some concept of property rights. If a member of a chimp group picks a piece of fruit, no other chimpanzee will try to take it away by force, even if the chimpanzee is the lowest-ranking member. Humans might have inherited ideas of ownership from their apelike ancestors. Scientists, however, disagree about whether property ideas are instinctive to human beings. In practice, ownership rights have to be enforced by laws and customs.

IS THIS YOURS?
In the past, many Native-American tribes had no concept of owning land. They might not own the reeds growing beside a lake, but if they harvested those reeds and wove them into a basket, that basket would belong to them.

HOME, SWEET HOME
Chinese property laws allowed Wu Ping to hold on to her house in the city of Chongqing even after all her neighbors had sold their property to a developer. She refused to move even when she found herself living on an isolated rock pillar in the middle of an enormous construction site. In the end, however, Wu Ping reached an agreement with the developer and the house was demolished.

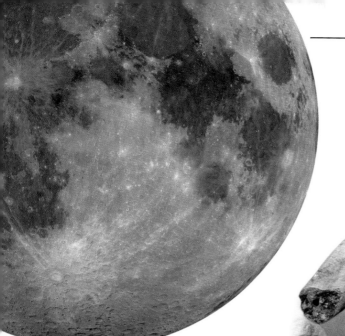

WHOSE TREASURE IS THIS?
The question of who owns something can become complicated. In 1801, British ambassador Thomas Elgin bought some Greek marble reliefs from the Turkish government that then ruled Athens. They are now in the British Museum, but the Greek government wants them back. The British argue that they paid for them and have looked after them for 200 years. Whose claim is valid?

A PIECE OF THE MOON
In 1967, the United Nations signed a treaty preventing any country from claiming ownership of the Moon and other areas of space. It did not say anything about individuals or corporations, however. Dennis Hope of Nevada has made millions of dollars by claiming parcels of land on the Moon and selling them. Buying them as an investment would be risky—Earthly courts may not respect Hope's claims—but they make interesting presents.

Bluefin tuna

TRAGEDY OF THE COMMONS
If no one owns a resource and everyone can use it, no one has any particular reason to care for it properly. Economists refer to this situation as "the tragedy of the commons." The fate of the bluefin tuna is a sad example. Under international law, no one owns the open ocean or the fish that live in it. This has resulted in a free-for-all—fishermen have hunted this tasty species to the verge of extinction.

THAT'S MY IDEA
Ideas can be at least as valuable as physical items. For much of history, people were free to use other people's ideas without paying for them. Many governments eventually decided that this was unfair. It was also harmful, because inventors were less likely to come up with useful new ideas if there were no guarantees that they would profit from them. Intellectual property laws were developed to protect inventors' ideas so that no one could steal them.

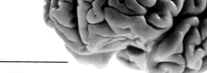

THIS LAND IS MY LAND
Communities with little or no concept of land ownership are sometimes forced to fight for the land they occupy if others threaten to take it over. These Native Americans of the Peruvian rain forest in South America assert their right to live on and use the land for hunting or farming, but may not make a legal claim to own it. Peru's laws allow land ownership, however, so logging companies can stake claim to forested land, which prevents the forest people from using it. Violent protests by Native Americans in 2009 led to the scrapping of two of Peru's land-ownership laws.

Division of labor

BY WORKING TOGETHER IN TEAMS, people can do far more than they could on their own. This is not just about some tasks being too difficult for one person, such as lifting an extremely heavy object. There are many jobs that can be done much more quickly together, particularly if they are broken down into stages, with different people responsible for each stage. This is because people who do a particular task again and again get better and faster at performing it and become specialists. They are more efficient and productive, which means that they do more work in an hour than nonspecialists. This process of dividing up a task to get the maximum work done in the least possible time is known as division of labor.

A HIVE OF ACTIVITY
Division of labor is not just a human activity—bees do it, too. Some worker bees collect nectar, others convert it into honey, and the rest guard the hive. Meanwhile, the queen bee does almost nothing but lay eggs. If all the bees tried to do everything, they would spend so much time moving between jobs that there would be chaos and far less honey would be produced.

Cell for storing food and eggs

SKILLED CRAFT
The development of agriculture freed people from having to look for food, giving them more time to specialize in other tasks and activities. As a result, far more goods were produced, and skilled crafts such as metalwork flourished. This bronze dragon head representing the Babylonian god Marduk is from 6th-century-BCE Mesopotamia.

18th-century engraving of a pin factory

Specialist places heads on pins

Fire lit to heat the metal

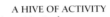

Pins

WORKING TOGETHER
The 18th-century economist Adam Smith believed that even simple tasks like the manufacture of pins could be performed more efficiently through cooperation and specialization. He calculated that 10 people could make as many pins in a given period of time as 2,400 working individually. However, specialization may lead to boredom. Workers can start to feel like machines, causing them to become unhappy and less productive.

Worker bee

Employee performs his specialized task

UNEQUAL REWARDS?
The 19th-century British inventor and industrialist Lord Armstrong, who owned this magnificent house, paid himself more than all his employees put together. Was this unfair? Many economists would say no. One worker could perhaps be replaced with another, but Armstrong's contribution was irreplaceable—without his inventions, their jobs would not have existed. It is often difficult to place a value on each person's contribution to a team effort.

ASSEMBLY LINE
Between 1908 and 1913, the Ford Motor Company perfected the assembly line, in which cars were built in successive stages via conveyor belts. These belts brought the work to specialized workers in exactly the right sequence, reducing the time taken to make a car from 12.5 hours to just over 1.5 hours. The resulting increase in productivity led to greater profits for the company, lower prices for buyers, and higher wages for employees.

Trade

THE EXCHANGE OF ONE THING for another is called trade. Individuals and businesses trade because they cannot produce something they want or need, or because it makes more sense for them to concentrate on producing other things. Someone without the equipment or skills to produce a television, for example, can buy it from a company that specializes in making them, trading money for the TV. Goods and services are increasingly traded across international borders, between individuals and companies in different countries. Goods and services leaving a country are called exports, and those entering are called imports. Some governments seek to protect their national industries from cheaper imports by imposing tariffs, which are taxes on goods imported from other countries.

FIRST TRADE
Flint tools discovered in areas where the stone does not naturally occur may be evidence of prehistoric trade. Sharp, chipped stone flints were used to build shelters, make clothes, and cut meat. People living in areas where this resource was not available most likely exchanged goods with people from other regions for a supply of their flint.

Rooster

Apples

SWAP SHOP
In the modern world, trade usually involves the exchange of goods or services for money, but before money was invented, items were exchanged directly, or bartered. An example of this is swapping a rooster for an agreed upon quantity of apples. The barter system continues alongside money to the present day. In fact, with the growth of trade in unwanted items between people in Internet communities, bartering is gaining in popularity.

Ship leaving Lisbon port, Portugal

LOCAL SPECIALTIES
Businesses in a country or region may specialize in producing particular goods and services because they use local natural resources or the area has become well known for businesses with expertise in that field. Filmmakers first moved to Hollywood, a district in Los Angeles, because its year-round sunny climate was perfect for outdoor filming. From just two movie studios in the 1910s, Hollywood is now the global center of the film industry.

GOING GLOBAL
Spices such as pepper and cardamom were highly prized in 15th- and 16th-century Europe. The traditional trade routes to the spice-rich islands of south and east Asia were controlled by Arab traders, and spices were very costly by the time they reached Europe. European explorers sailed the globe in search of new routes to the spice islands, and over time silks and spices from the east and precious metals and sugar from the west became major sources of wealth for European nations.

Cardamom

PLAYGROUND TRADING
Trade involves the exchange of goods and services so that people can satisfy their wants. Everyone engages in trade in some form or the other in their everyday life. Even swapping cards among friends is a form of trade.

BREAKING DOWN BARRIERS
Sometimes a government tries to protect its country's industries by setting up barriers to trade, such as tariffs, against competing nations. Some nations are also part of trade blocs, where tariffs are reduced or eliminated between member countries. For example, people, goods, and services can move freely between the 27 countries belonging to the European Union.

European
Union flag

GLOBAL IMPACT
In today's interlinked world, events or decisions made in one country can have major effects on the economies of other nations. If oil-producing nations restrict their supply of oil, its global price rises. Many industries and forms of transportation are dependent on oil, so increased costs have a huge impact on worldwide trade.

A tanker transports
oil between nations

The birth of money

BEFORE PEOPLE STARTED USING MONEY, they used the barter, or exchange, system to obtain goods. One drawback, however, was its inefficiency—a person who wanted to exchange a goat for some firewood might not easily find a person who wanted to exchange firewood for a goat. The invention of money provided a solution to this problem. As its value was recognized by everyone, people could buy and sell whatever they wanted quickly and easily. Money had to be relatively scarce if it was to preserve its value, but not too scarce, or most people would still have to engage in barter (imagine a city with only two coins). It also had to be difficult to fake, portable, long-lasting, and easily divisible.

ROARING SUCCESS
Metal was a popular ancient form of commodity money. The problem with accepting it as payment was establishing how pure it was. The world's first coins—minted in Lydia (present-day Turkey) around 640 BCE—solved this problem. They were stamped with the king's lion-head symbol as a guarantee of their purity.

Barley grain

EVERY GRAIN MATTERS
In ancient Mesopotamia, the shekel was the basic unit of both weight and currency. A shekel originally consisted of 180 grains of barley. Forms of money based on items that are useful in themselves, such as barley, metal, or salt, are known as commodity money.

Symbols indicate that this 14th-century Chinese note is equivalent to 1,000 coins

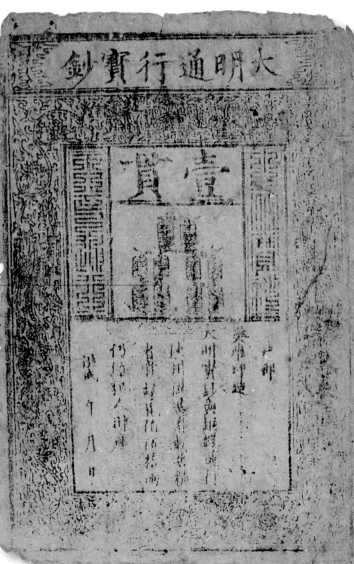

大明通行寶鈔

壹

貫

Currency beads

Cowrie shells

MONEY BEADS
Many objects have been used as currency through the ages, such as beads, cowrie shells, and ring-shaped stones. Almost anything can serve as currency, provided that people agree to accept it as payment for goods and services.

Ring coin

Beads

NOTEWORTHY EVENT
In 10th-century China, people started to leave their heavy iron coins with merchants. The merchants gave handwritten receipts in return, and the people began using the receipts as money. Eventually, the government took over from the merchants and printed receipts that could be used officially as money. These were the first banknotes—the first paper currency.

GOLD STANDARD

For centuries, the values of coins and paper currency were linked to specified quantities of gold. Known as the "gold standard," this meant a country's wealth was linked to the size of its gold reserves. The system helped simplify international trade, since payments in gold were acceptable everywhere.

This figure indicates the value of the money

Serial number identifies the note and helps prevent theft and forgery

Tunisian dinar banknotes and coins

LET IT BE MONEY

In 1971, countries the world over abandoned linking the value of their currencies to gold. Today's coins and banknotes have value only because governments say they do. This form of money is known as fiat money, which comes from the Latin *fiat*, meaning "let it be done."

Microchip holds information about the card holder

Holograms are difficult to reproduce and help prevent forgery

Aragonite stone is a form of limestone

FLASH CASH

Most transactions today are done using "virtual money." No physical money changes hands at all. Instead, digits are moved from computer to computer. Pieces of plastic, such as the debit cards above, are used to hold account details and certify identity. When a person uses a debit card to buy something, money is moved directly from their bank account into the account of the seller.

ROCK MARKET

Prior to the 20th century, the people of the Pacific island of Yap used enormous aragonite stone disks as money. Called *rai*, they often weighed several tons, and the largest ones were more than 10 ft (3 m) in diameter. They were almost impossible to move around, so people just had to remember who owned which one. Fortunately though, they also had smaller coins for daily use.

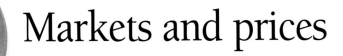

Markets and prices

HOW DO THE PRICES OF THINGS get decided? Sometimes they are set by governments, or by monopolies, which are companies that have complete control over the sale of certain products. The most common way prices are decided, however, is through markets. These are forums where buyers and sellers meet—from street markets and shopping malls to Internet auctions and stock market trading rooms. In a market, prices emerge as individual deals are made. Products get sold when buyers and sellers agree on prices. Goods in plentiful supply in relation to consumer demand tend to settle at lower prices than sought-after rarer products.

MONOPOLIES
When a government or company controls the sale of an item, it has a monopoly. It can charge what it wants, so buyers may have to pay high prices. In 1596, a royal monopoly on salt in the state of Bavaria accounted for 40 percent of the ruler's revenue.

THE MARKETPLACE
A key feature of markets is competition. In a busy street market, buyers and sellers can easily find out the prices on offer at every stall. This allows them to compare and make choices. Provided there are plenty of buyers and sellers, everyone has a chance to make transactions at prices they are happy with.

Outdoor market at Kota Bharu, Malaysia

SETTING PRICES
In many stores, sellers decide on the prices of their goods in advance and use labels to advertise them. There is usually no room for negotiation. If a product fails to sell, however, the seller is likely to lower its price to attract more customers. If it sells out rapidly, the seller may raise the price, since the demand for it suggests buyers might pay more.

SELLING TO THE HIGHEST BIDDER
This picture shows an auction in London, England, in 1808. In an auction, there is no fixed price. Instead, items are sold to whoever bids the highest price for them. If many people want to buy a unique object like an old painting, its sale price will be high. But if only one person wants it, the price will stay low.

NEGOTIATING PRICES
Two Moroccan men haggle (negotiate) over a camel. The seller has a minimum price he will accept but hopes to get more, while the buyer has a maximum price he will pay but hopes to pay less. If they can both agree upon a price, the camel will be sold.

COSTLY, RICH, AND RARE
Diamonds are expensive because they are rare and desirable objects. Their supply is low, while demand for them is high. If things people want badly or need urgently are in short supply, buyers will be prepared to pay very high prices to make sure they obtain them.

TOO MUCH OF A GOOD THING
If car makers produce more cars than people are willing to buy at current prices, then, in economic terms, supply is greater than demand. To get rid of their excess stock, manufacturers have to reduce car prices to persuade people to buy them. This is how markets handle gluts, which are the opposite of shortages.

GOING CRAZY OVER TULIPS
If people expect the price of a product to rise, there will be an increase in demand as investors buy more of it in the hope of selling it later for a profit. This can lead to unstable prices. In the Netherlands in the 17th century, tulips became so popular that single bulbs sold for more than 10 times a skilled worker's yearly wages, but then the tulip market collapsed and the bulbs were worth little.

VIRTUAL MARKETS
Markets are not always physical places. On the Internet, buyers and sellers can meet in virtual marketplaces including auction sites, such as eBay, and comparison sites that analyze hundreds of competing online stores and services. The Internet hosts many specialized markets, but in some ways, all the world's Internet users combine to make up a single giant market.

Banking

Banks serve as safe places for people to keep their money. But the money deposited in banks by their customers does not sit in a safe. Banks take most of their depositors' money and lend it to borrowers, who use it for things like starting or expanding businesses and purchasing homes. Banks are able to do this because they know that it is unlikely that all of their depositors will want to take out all of their money at the same time. Banks make money by charging borrowers a percentage of the money they lend them. These charges are known as interest. They also insist that the original sum borrowed is eventually paid back. Of course, banks do not want to lend money to people who they think may not pay it back, so they charge higher interest rates for loans they consider risky. They also try to lend funds to businesses with the most promising projects, leading to benefits for the whole economy.

SAFE PLACE
In some ways, temples such as this one in the ancient city of Hatra, Iraq, were the first banks. People stored their valuables in temples because they trusted the temple guardians to look after them well (for a fee). In time, people started accepting temple receipts—which were issued to get back deposits—as payment for other goods.

Early banknotes

Coins

Banker's notebook

BANKING ON A BENCH
European banking took off in Italy in the 12th and 13th centuries. In centers of trade such as Genoa, Venice, and Florence, moneylenders would set up their tables and benches in open spaces such as market squares. If a moneylender ran out of money, his bench was broken to let people know. "A broken bench" is *una banca rotta* in Italian, and the origin of the English word bankrupt.

The Medici family coat of arms

Crossed keys refer to the Medici popes

THE WEALTHIEST BANKERS
Between the 14th and 16th centuries, pioneering banking families such as the Medici in Florence, Italy, became wealthy by lending money to profitable businesses. The Medici grew to be very powerful, eventually becoming rulers of Florence. They were also patrons of the arts, and paid for some of the greatest paintings and sculptures ever seen, employing famous artists such as Michelangelo and Leonardo da Vinci. Three members of the Medici family even became pope. The family coat of arms is still displayed on many buildings in Florence.

Balls may represent coins

Crest of Pope Leo XI, born Alessandro Ottaviano de' Medici

MONEYLENDERS
This old painting from a museum in Bilbao, Spain, shows a moneylender going through his accounts. Moneylenders made money by charging fees and interest on loans. Before modern banking came about, moneylenders played an important economic role. They were not very popular, though. Some religions forbade lending money, so it was often done by religious outsiders.

WORTHY OF A LOAN?

WORTHY OF A LOAN?
Banks do not want to lend money to people who might not be able to pay it back. They need to be convinced that would-be borrowers are reliable and have good business plans. Philip Knight and Bill Bowerman, the founders of Nike, could begin importing Japanese sports shoes into the US only after they persuaded the First National Bank of Portland to give them a 90-day loan.

Nike shoes

INTEREST RATES
Farmers in 19th-century New Mexico practiced a system called partido. If a farmer lent a flock of sheep to a neighbor, he would expect it to be returned after a year, along with an agreed to percentage of the lambs born during that period. Modern banks similarly set interest rates on all loans they grant. Banks also pay interest to reward customers who save money. Interest rates affect economies because when they are high, people borrow less and save more. When they are low, people usually borrow more and save less.

MODERN BANKING
In addition to lending out depositors' savings to individuals and businesses, modern banks make investments of their own. Sometimes they specialize in activities such as helping companies to buy other companies, or selling insurance. In many cities, banks and related businesses cluster together in one area, such as Wall Street in New York City and the financial district of Hong Kong, shown in this picture.

Bank of China Tower

Citibank Plaza

Savings and investments

SAVING MEANS PUTTING MONEY ASIDE instead of spending it all at once. People save for a "rainy day" when money may be scarce, or to allow them to make expensive purchases in the future. Saving is low risk—money in a bank account is unlikely to grow a great deal in value, but it will be safe. Investment is riskier. It involves purchasing assets (items of value) in the hope that they will be worth more over time and provide returns (profits). Assets include shares in companies (see pages 30–31) and capital—money, equipment, and buildings used to generate wealth. Often people borrow money from banks to finance investments.

WHY SAVE?
In an unpredictable world, savings are a cushion against hard times and emergencies. Just as squirrels hoard nuts to see them through winters without food, people put money aside for future purchases as well as for unexpected expenses. People also save for their retirement, when they will no longer be earning a salary.

WHY INVEST?
Money stashed under a mattress or in a jar at home could get stolen, but the biggest problem is that it will not grow in value. Indeed, if prices rise, it will actually be worth less. People make investments in the hope of making more money. This means eventually getting back more money than they paid.

Giant robotic arm welds car frame together

INVESTING IN MACHINES
At this Hyundai factory in Beijing, China, robotic arms weld car frames together. Complicated machinery like these robots is expensive, but in the long run the company expects to see a good return on its investment. This is because it costs less to buy robots to do certain tasks, such as welding, than it would cost to pay humans to do those tasks.

313-

HX165-02

PROFITS FROM PROPERTY

Individuals can make all kinds of personal investments, including putting their money into shares of companies (see pages 34–35) and buying property or land. For most homeowners, the biggest investment they will make in their lives is buying a house. As a bonus, they get to live in it while it (hopefully) increases in value.

Part of the Bonneville Dam on the Columbia River in Oregon

TOP SAVERS

China has one of the highest savings rates in the world. This is partly because people have to pay for their own health care, education, and retirement, and also because saving is encouraged in Chinese culture. The more a country saves, the more it can invest, and the more its economy grows.

Chinese coins, an ancient symbol of wealth

INVESTING FOR EVERYONE

Governments make investments, too. They use the money they raise through taxes to pay for public projects such as dams, roads, bridges, and power plants. These projects are designed to benefit everyone and boost the economy. Building a new bridge, for example, can considerably reduce transportation costs for local businesses. It can also increase trade, as people from outside gain access to the area.

Visitors with Mickey and Minnie Mouse at Tokyo Disneyland, Japan

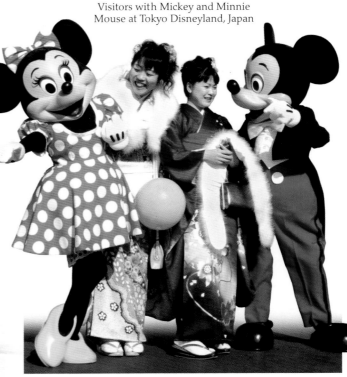

WORLDWIDE REACH

Investors choose between companies and economies all over the world. When making their decisions, they try to balance risk (the chance of things not turning out as expected) with the highest potential rates of return. The Walt Disney Company has invested in theme parks in Europe and Asia, making it a multinational business.

Currencies and exchange rates

MOST COUNTRIES HAVE THEIR own form of money—their own paper money and coins—known as their currency. When people go on vacation to another country, they need to change their money into the currency of the country they are visiting. Tourists buy the foreign money with their own country's currency at a certain price, called the exchange rate. The exchange rate changes every day, because like most prices, it is determined by a market—a market of currency buyers and sellers. For example, if everyone wants Indian rupees, this currency will become more expensive. If no one wants US dollars, they will become cheaper. Governments often try to control exchange rates. They might buy and sell currencies themselves or limit the flow of money into and out of the country. They might even fix the exchange rate by matching their currency's value to another one, usually the US dollar.

COSTLY IMPORTS
When a country buys more goods and services from other countries than it sells to them, the exchange rate of its currency tends to fall. Bangladesh, for instance, imports huge amounts of rice each year. This puts strong downward pressure on the exchange value of its money, because it must convert a lot of local currency into foreign currency to pay foreign producers for their rice.

FOR A FEW DOLLARS MORE
Most foreign-exchange trading occurs in the big financial centers, such as the New York, London, and Tokyo stock exchanges. These markets do business worth more than 1 trillion (million million) dollars a day. Some of this trade involves banks, companies, and governments buying and selling currencies, but most of the trading is done by currency speculators. These traders make informed guesses about the future values of currencies and generate a profit when their predictions come true.

Pile of Indian one-rupee coins needed to buy one pound sterling

CHANGING VALUES
When the markets determine the value of a country's currency, the country is said to have a floating exchange rate. The Indian rupee has a floating exchange rate and its value compared to other currencies changes daily. Over longer periods, exchange rates can change dramatically. In 2001, 90 US cents would buy 1 euro, but in 2008, 1 euro cost $1.47.

VACATION MONEY

People traveling abroad need the currency of the country they are visiting to spend on living expenses and souvenirs, such as these Russian nesting dolls. Bureaux de change (foreign-exchange offices) buy and sell travelers' currencies. They are often located at banks, travel agencies, and airports. They make a profit by charging a commission (transaction fee), and by selling currencies for a higher price than what they paid to buy them.

STREET DEALS

If a government fixes the exchange rate of its currency, a "black market," or illegal market, in the currency can emerge. This happens because the government-fixed value of the currency is often too high or too low, and traders turn to illegal dealers to get a better price. These Afghan traders are selling the national currency—the afghani—on the streets of the capital, Kabul.

MONEY KNOWS NO BORDERS

Changing currencies all the time is costly, and the uncertainty over ever-changing prices also costs businesses money. To eliminate these problems, the governments of most countries belonging to the European Union have opted for currency union, adopting a single currency called the euro. The disadvantage of currency union is that the member countries cannot have separate policies to deal with their specific financial problems.

PEGGING CURRENCY

Some governments choose a fixed exchange rate over a floating one to stabilize their economies and make international trade more predictable. Malaysia fixed, or "pegged," the value of its currency—the ringgit—to the US dollar during a period of financial uncertainty between 1998 and 2005.

Companies and corporations

A **COMPANY OR CORPORATION** is formed when a group of people get together to make or sell something as a team. For most companies, earning maximum profits is the goal. Profit is the sum of money left over when all of a company's spending has been accounted for. The key advantage of forming a company rather than producing something as an individual is economies of scale—the more items made, the lower the cost to produce. Transaction expenses (buying and selling costs) are also reduced if they happen within an organization. If the owners of a company want to raise funds for new projects, they may sell shares, or parts of the company. Shareholders may own stakes in the business, but it is run by a board of directors.

TOP DOG
A company with a chain of hot-dog stands can sell more than a single salesperson. Buying ingredients in large amounts means the hot-dog company can also strike better deals with suppliers. This in turn can lead to greater profits for the company.

Spire on top of five-story pagoda

One of three gates to the pagoda

RECORD BREAKER
Prior to being taken over by the Takamatsu Corporation in 2006, the Kongo Gumi construction firm of Osaka, Japan, was the oldest company in the world. It could trace its origins back to 578 CE. The firm specialized in building Japanese temples, such as Osaka's Shitenno-ji Buddhist temple, shown here.

Coat of arms of British East India Company

LEGAL SAFEGUARDS
If a company has "limited liability," its shareholders are not legally responsible for paying its debts if it goes bust. This arrangement, which encourages firms to invest and take commercial risks, helped the British East India Company become the richest company of the 18th century, trading in goods from the areas of India it controlled.

BBC Broadcasting House, London, UK

FOR THE PUBLIC GOOD
Most companies exist to make profits, which are then distributed to their owners or shareholders. Some companies, however, exist solely to provide services for the benefit of the public, or to promote particular values or beliefs. Nonprofit organizations such as the British Broadcasting Corporation (BBC) are legally required to plow any profits they make back into their businesses.

IN CHARGE
On a day-to-day basis, a company is run by its chief executive and managers. The people who oversee their activities are known as the directors. Collectively called the board, directors are responsible for the general direction the company takes and for ensuring that its finances are in good order. If a company has shareholders, they have a say in who the directors are, while in privately owned companies, the owners appoint the directors.

BIG BUSINESS
Companies with operations in more than one country are called multinational companies. Coca-Cola, for example, has manufacturing and bottling plants in more than 100 countries. This global empire worth $100 billion is run from the company headquarters in Atlanta, Georgia.

An African tribesman drinking Coca-Cola

Google founders Larry Page, and Sergey Brin (right)

COMPANY CULTURE
The kind of culture a company looks to create for its workers or staff can be crucial to its success. The offices of the Internet search engine firm Google are filled with leisure facilities that create a relaxed atmosphere designed to help employees to think creatively.

A General Motors car sold under the German brand, Opel

RISKY BUSINESS
Most companies seek to grow in order to sell more of whatever they produce and make greater profits. Some rely on coming up with new business. Others expand by buying rival companies and merging with them. This can be a risky policy. The US car manufacturer General Motors became huge by acquiring other car companies, such as Opel in Europe. But with too many different brands under one roof, the company lost its focus and went bankrupt in 2009.

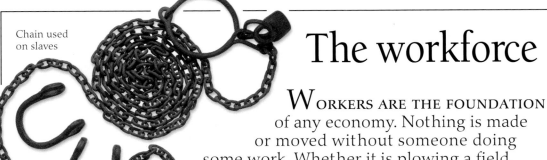

Chain used on slaves

The workforce

WORKERS ARE THE FOUNDATION of any economy. Nothing is made or moved without someone doing some work. Whether it is plowing a field, typing a letter, or designing a house, it is all work. In most of the world today, work is organized through the market. It is paid for with wages, and employees are given legal contracts. Workers with rare skills or those who are organized into trade unions may be able to raise their wages. Where workers' skills are commonplace and demand for them is low, they may have to accept lower wages, or even face unemployment.

SLAVE LABOR
A slave is a person who is owned and treated like a piece of property. Slave labor was a feature of many historical economies, including those of ancient Greece and Rome, medieval Europe, and the US in the 18th and 19th centuries. Today, slavery is outlawed in almost every country.

Coat of arms of the Society of Pewterers, New York City, 1788

Pewter coffee pot

SOLID AND PURE

WORKERS' GUILDS
In some preindustrial economies, skilled workers—such as tailors and goldsmiths—banded together to form guilds. The state often gave these organizations powers and coats of arms. The guilds controlled who could join and practice their trades, the rules and regulations of the trades, and often the prices their members could charge for work.

Banner showing "a monkey wrench in the works" to symbolize industrial protest

Protest by German employees of a car manufacturer

Clenched fist symbolizes the workers' strength and unity

Assembling laptops at an electronics factory in Shenzhen, China

WHOSE HARVEST?

This Thai woman is gathering in the rice harvest. More than 40 percent of the world's workers are involved in agriculture, and most are landless peasants who work for a small class of wealthy landowners. Some peasants are allowed to rent land from the owner. In return, they must hand over a share of their harvest, or work on the landowner's estate.

SUPPLY AND DEMAND

In a market economy, labor has its price. Workers sell their time and skills, and employers buy these with wages. Where labor is scarce, wages tend to rise. When labor is plentiful, as in modern China, its price falls. One reason why China's economy has grown so fast in recent years is that it has a huge supply of workers, keeping wages low. This means that products can be manufactured very cheaply in China.

Architect using his design, building, and communication skills in the workplace

WORKERS' RIGHTS

Trade unions grew out of the collective efforts of workers to defend their interests at work. In developing countries, trade unions often fight against harsh conditions and low wages. In rich societies, they may be strong enough to push for higher wages. Trade unions use a variety of strategies to achieve their goals, such as negotiation and discussion with employers and governments, fighting workers' cases in court, and public protests. They may even organize a strike—a mass withdrawal of labor.

Red flag has been used by workers' groups for more than a century

SKILLED WORKFORCE

Why do architects earn more than construction workers? It is again a matter of supply and demand. There is always a strong demand for architects and construction workers because we are constantly putting up new buildings. But since the training to be an architect takes nearly a decade, there are far fewer architects than construction workers. Employers therefore have to pay more for their services.

LABOR LAWS

This Mexican woman works in a factory as a welder—a job once reserved exclusively for men. Governments now pass laws to make it illegal to refuse people jobs or pay different wage rates on the grounds of gender, race, or disability. The state may also set minimum wage rates to prevent poor people from being exploited.

Shares and bonds

Two of the most popular ways of investing money are buying shares and buying bonds. When people buy shares in a company, they become part owners of it. If the value of the company rises, the shares become more valuable, and if it falls, the shares decline in value. The company's directors may also decide to pay shareholders a proportion, known as a dividend, of any profits the company makes. People who buy a company's bonds do not become its part owners. Instead, they are lending it money. In return, the company promises to pay them interest (loan fees) at regular intervals, and to repay the original sum at an agreed upon future date. Governments also issue bonds to raise money. These are seen as less risky than bonds issued by companies, since governments are unlikely to go bankrupt, so they usually pay lower rates of interest.

GOING PUBLIC
If a company wants its shares to be traded on a stock market, it sells them to the public in what is known as a flotation, or initial public offering (IPO). This share certificate was issued by the International Steam Pump Company of New Jersey on its flotation in 1909. Some people specialize in buying shares through IPOs, hoping to sell them quickly for a profit. Known as "stags," they often succeed because companies tend to sell their shares at a low price initially to make sure they all get sold.

TAKING STOCK
A stock exchange is a market in which people buy and sell shares in companies. Today, there are huge buildings in cities all over the world, as well as several websites, dedicated to these activities. Before stock exchanges were established, however, there were no fixed places where people could go to buy and sell shares. In 18th-century London, share dealers used to conduct their business in coffee houses.

BULLS
People who expect the value of shares to rise are known as bulls. The term has been used to describe positive or optimistic share dealers since the early 18th century. Like the animals they are named after, these people charge forward fearlessly, buying shares in the expectation that they will increase in value. If this happens, they will be able to sell them for a profit. A stock market in which prices are rising overall is known as a bull market.

Bull ornament from a stock trader's office

MADE TO MEASURE

The rising and falling values of shares on this screen can be summed up by a single number called a stock market index. The index measures the average value of a fixed selection of shares in a market, and it changes constantly every day. Investors can measure how well their shares are performing compared to the index. The Dow Jones Industrial Average index tracks the share prices of 30 of the largest companies in the US, and the NASDAQ index charts the performance of many leading technology companies.

RAISING FUNDS FOR LIBERTY

Governments sometimes issue bonds to raise money for financing development projects or to fund costly wars. This is a poster for Liberty Bonds, which were issued by the US government between 1917 and 1918 to help raise finances during World War I. They paid investors between 3.5 and 4.5 percent interest per year.

A SHARE OF THE MARKET

An IPO, in which people buy shares directly from a company, is an example of what is known as a primary market. In secondary markets people buy and sell shares, usually on behalf of other people. These markets can be extremely busy places—these traders and clerks are signaling prices at the Mercantile Exchange in Chicago. There is lots of shouting and hand waving as the traders try to attract the attention of other traders to enable them to negotiate prices and buy and sell shares.

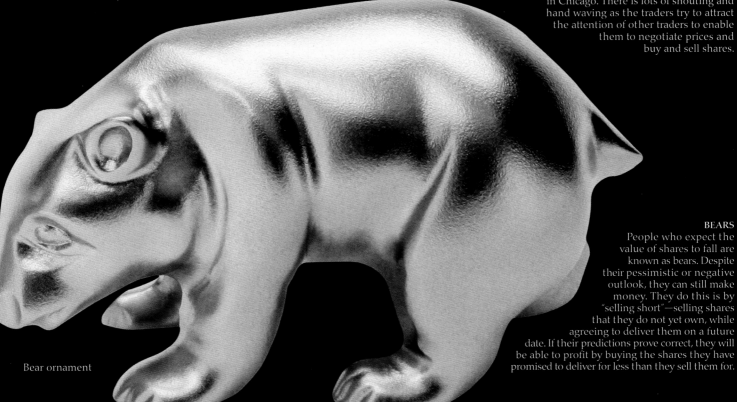

BEARS

People who expect the value of shares to fall are known as bears. Despite their pessimistic or negative outlook, they can still make money. They do this is by "selling short"—selling shares that they do not yet own, while agreeing to deliver them on a future date. If their predictions prove correct, they will be able to profit by buying the shares they have promised to deliver for less than they sell them for.

Bear ornament

Speculation

THE LURE OF MAKING LARGE PROFITS can lead people to stake their money, or bet, on risky investments and business deals. This is known as speculation. People who speculate make bets on the expected future prices of assets—such as shares, land, or even antiques—in the hope of making a big profit. Speculators can bet on the price of something falling as well as rising. Either way, if things go as they predict, they end up with more money than they began with. Otherwise, they may be in trouble, particularly if they have borrowed money to place their bets. While investors are concerned with putting their money to productive use over the long term to earn profits, speculators take a chance with their money in the hope of larger-than-normal gains. Speculation can influence markets, too, leading to price swings and financial crises. For instance, if speculators start investing in property, expecting house prices to rise, this demand will itself cause house prices to increase, leading to a runaway housing boom.

GOLD RUSH
In 1848, traces of gold were found in the water used by a lumber mill in Coloma, California. Hundreds of thousands of people from across the US and all over the world flocked to California to look for gold. The discovery led to furious speculation in the local property market—people bought and sold land where gold was thought to exist. Fortunes were made, particularly by those who had arrived early on the scene, but many people lost money, too, especially when the gold started to run out. Nevertheless, the gold rush had a permanent effect on the California economy, creating new markets and swelling the population of the state from 100,000 to 380,000 within a span of just 10 years.

Share trader   *Potential investor*

THE SOUTH SEA BUBBLE
In 1720, Britain was gripped by stock market fever. The South Sea Bubble was triggered by the government granting the South Sea Company sole rights to trade with South America. Its share price quickly shot up, and the boom in the market sparked a buying frenzy for other shares, once South Sea shares were no longer available. The bubble finally burst when the company did not earn as much profit from its trade as was expected. Many people were ruined as share prices plunged. The painting above shows trading of shares in London's Exchange Alley during that period.

ACCIDENTAL GAMBLE

Speculation can be beneficial at times. Insurance companies promise to cover customers' costs if they are victims of theft, bad health, or accidents. It is a gamble, because they might have to make a big payment for a serious accident or costly illness. Each customer makes regular small payments to the insurer, and because the insurance companies receive small payments from many people, they can afford to make a few big payments. However, if they miscalculate how much money they will have to pay out, they can lose money.

COLLAPSE OF A BANK

A trader making a rogue (unauthorized) speculation can cause an enormous amount of damage. In 1995, the 232-year-old UK Barings Bank collapsed after an employee lost $1.3 billion on the stock markets. Without telling his bosses, Nick Leeson invested a large amount of the bank's funds, betting that prices on the Japanese stock market would not change much overnight. Unfortunately, Japan was hit by a massive earthquake and share prices plummeted. Leeson was charged with fraud for deceiving the bank and spent four years in prison in Singapore.

BETTING ON THE OUTCOME

The price of a property (or any asset that is bought and then resold) is affected by what people think it will be worth in the future. However, if a speculator believes that the current price underestimates a property's future value, they will want to buy that property so that they will profit when its value rises higher than most people thought it would. Gambling at a racetrack is a kind of speculation. Gamblers place a bet on a horse that they think will do well. If the bookmakers (the people or company taking the bet) do not expect the horse to win, they offer a high price for a winning bet, and the gambler gets a lot of money in return if the horse finishes first.

Racing jockey

Booms and busts

ECONOMIC ACTIVITY HAS ITS PEAKS and valleys. An increase in economic activity, with new businesses opening up and people making lots of money, may lead to a period of boom. This is often followed by a period of bust, when the economy slows down, resulting in companies going out of business and people losing their jobs. When such a period persists for a long time, the economy is said to be in a recession. Booms and busts are often triggered by dramatic changes in the economy, such as the invention of new technology or crop failure. Neither boom nor bust is considered good because each leads to instability in the long run. Instead, governments strive for a steady and continuous rate of economic growth.

HERD BEHAVIOR
In 1873, the New York Stock Exchange crashed when the bank funding the Northern Pacific Railroad Project collapsed. Since many people had invested money in the expansion of the American railroad network, panic spread through the market and share prices fell sharply. People withdrew their money from the bank and tried to sell their shares, following each other like sheep following the herd.

People running out of the New York Stock Exchange following its crash in 1873

MAKING CONNECTIONS
In the 1920s, technology such as the radio and telephone made communication easier and swifter. These developments enabled people to do more business than they had done before, which quickly led to an economic boom, often called the "Roaring Twenties." This picture shows a 1920s telephone made of Bakelite (an early plastic).

THE GREAT DEPRESSION
A depression is an extreme form of recession, in which economic activity decreases dramatically and millions of people lose their jobs. During the Great Depression of the 1930s, global economic output fell by one-third and unemployment reached 25 percent or higher in all the major economies. The biggest depression in history, it was triggered by the Wall Street Crash of 1929, when share prices suddenly collapsed. Wall Street is the location of the New York Stock Exchange and center of New York City's financial district.

Unemployed men line up for free food at a soup kitchen in New York City during the Great Depression

NOT CHILD'S PLAY

Recessions and depressions are painful events, but often have positive consequences in the long run. Weak businesses go under, and old ways of doing things are replaced by more efficient methods. Japan was bankrupt at the end of World War II in 1945, but this spurred the country to start afresh. The Japanese economy grew amazingly quickly between the 1960s and 1980s. Among its biggest success stories is the toy industry.

Japanese toy robot

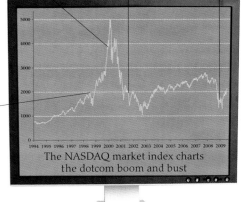

Sharp increase shows boom period

Sharp decline shows market going bust

2008–2009 recession

Market growing at a steady pace

The NASDAQ market index charts the dotcom boom and bust

THE DOTCOM CRASH

In the 1990s, Internet firms were the subject of an enormous speculative bubble, which led to a rise in stock prices of computer- and Internet-related companies. The Internet offered many new business possibilities, but investors got overexcited and put more money into information technology (IT) firms than they could possibly expect to earn back. People lost billions in the so-called "dotcom crash."

TIGER ECONOMIES

These ships belong to Samsung Heavy Industries, which is one of South Korea's most successful companies. The shipbuilding industry has contributed greatly to the country's economic boom in recent years. Many Asian economies experienced similar booms in the 1980s and early and mid-1990s. They are collectively known as "tiger economies."

These bulk-carrier ships are a sign of a booming South Korean economy

Credit crunch

THE MONEY THAT SAVERS deposit in banks is lent to individuals and businesses. If borrowers fail to repay, banks start running out of money. They reduce their lending to ensure they have enough money on hand to repay any savers who wish to withdraw their cash. People cannot borrow money if banks stop lending—a situation called a credit crunch. Modern economies run on borrowing, from families buying houses to businesses building factories, so a shortage of funds for lending makes the whole economy suffer. In 2008, a worldwide credit crunch was set off by banks lending too much money to people who had little chance of repaying it. Governments had to spend huge amounts to bail out the banks and to prevent their nations' economies from collapsing. Taxpayers will be paying for this for years to come.

FALLING SHARES
The credit crunch caused financial markets to crash all over the world. This created problems for businesses that wanted to raise money by issuing new shares, since it meant they would receive much less money for them. Pensions and savings funds are often invested on the stock market to increase their value, so falling share prices also left many millions of savers worse off.

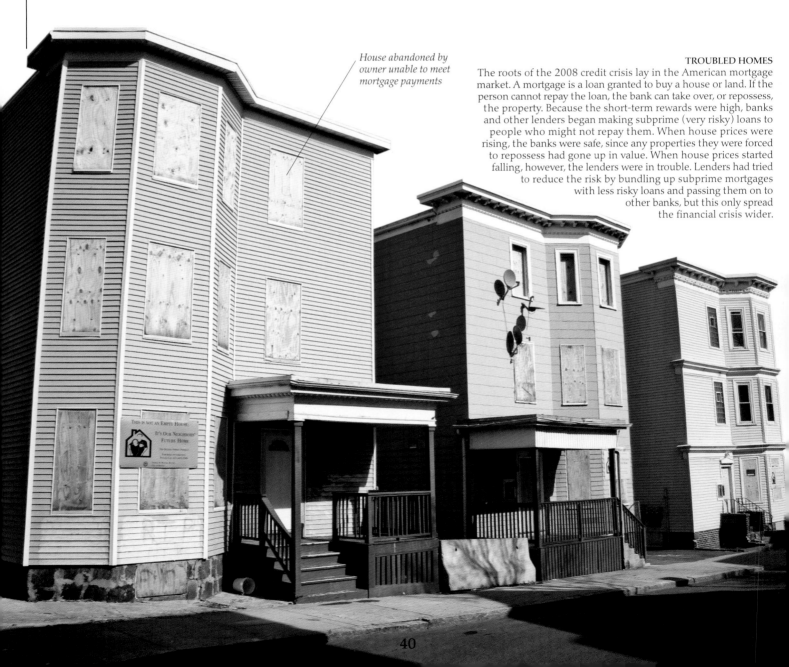

House abandoned by owner unable to meet mortgage payments

TROUBLED HOMES
The roots of the 2008 credit crisis lay in the American mortgage market. A mortgage is a loan granted to buy a house or land. If the person cannot repay the loan, the bank can take over, or repossess, the property. Because the short-term rewards were high, banks and other lenders began making subprime (very risky) loans to people who might not repay them. When house prices were rising, the banks were safe, since any properties they were forced to repossess had gone up in value. When house prices started falling, however, the lenders were in trouble. Lenders had tried to reduce the risk by bundling up subprime mortgages with less risky loans and passing them on to other banks, but this only spread the financial crisis wider.

A laid-off worker from Lehman Brothers leaves the office

A COUNTRY GOES BANKRUPT
The economy of Iceland was hit particularly badly by the credit crisis, since the small north Atlantic nation had specialized in high-risk banking practices. Before they collapsed, the country's three biggest banks had combined debts of more than six times Iceland's GDP (see pages 44–45). This forced the Icelandic government to resign, and caused the value of the country's currency to fall by more than two-thirds.

GOVERNMENT TO THE RESCUE
On September 13, 2007, long lines formed outside branches of UK bank Northern Rock amid rumors that the bank was in trouble. Customers withdrew almost $2 billion in a single day, leading the government to announce it was guaranteeing all Northern Rock deposits. Six months later, the bank was nationalized (taken over by the government). During the credit crunch, governments the world over rescued banks by lending them money to repay depositors.

BANKRUPT BANKS
In September 2008, the US investment bank Lehman Brothers filed for bankruptcy after it ran up debts of more than $600 billion. Although the company had assets worth many billions, it was unable to sell enough of them to meet its interest repayments. This led to the biggest corporate failure in American history, and thousands of employees were left jobless.

US Treasury Secretary Timothy Geithner

US President Barack Obama

TIGHTER CHECKS
One of the main causes of the credit crisis was governments failing to keep a check on large banks. Without strict regulation, banks got involved in risky activities that could cause great economic damage. They encouraged risk-taking by awarding their employees with huge bonuses if they hit certain targets, and lent money to companies and individuals who had little chance of paying it back. In the future, banks may have to keep a greater reserve of money for emergencies. Representatives from the US and other developed economies meet frequently to agree on new international solutions for the financial sector.

Poster advertising a going-out-of-business sale

THE CRUNCH HURTS
In today's interlinked economy, problems in one area can rapidly extend to others. This is what happened during the 2008 credit crisis. The difficulties of a few mortgage lenders that had specialized in extremely risky loans in the hope of greater profits caused a chain reaction that led to difficulties for almost every kind of business. To make up for their losses, banks decided to reduce or call back their loans, forcing many businesses into bankruptcy.

The role of governments

FROM PROTECTING NATIONAL BORDERS and building roads to providing education for the young and welfare support for the needy, governments tend to take on tasks that are difficult or dangerous to entrust to private individuals and companies. Maintaining a police force is always a government responsibility, because an individual might use it for personal gain instead of protecting the public. Governments also step in to provide basic necessities such as food, clothing, and shelter to people who cannot pay for these themselves. Private individuals and companies must make a profit, so they cannot fulfill these roles. Governments undertake these tasks because the law gives them the power to do so, and they fund their activities by collecting taxes.

GIVE US OUR DAILY BREAD
Governments may subsidize (bear part of the cost of) essential items like food to make sure they are affordable for everyone. The Egyptian government subsidizes the manufacture of bread. If it did not, many of the country's poor people might not be able to buy enough food.

FREE EDUCATION
In most countries, governments provide free education to create a skilled and literate workforce. This enables families, who would not otherwise be able to afford it, to send their children to school. These schoolchildren in Vietnam get free primary education. In most developed countries, education is free until students reach college.

PEOPLE'S WELFARE
Governments take different welfare measures to protect the health and well-being of their citizens—they may use taxes to fund hospitals, or provide payments to unemployed people. Some developed countries have special provisions for their senior citizens. They take care of their aged by building nursing homes, paying pensions, and providing free medical care.

NATIONAL SECURITY
Even if some businesses and individuals could afford to run private armies, it would be dangerous for governments to allow this to happen, because it could lead to power struggles or civil wars. The salaries, uniforms, and equipment of these US Army cadets are paid for by the US government.

BUILDING E
The Akashi-
12,831 ft (3,
carries six la
making it th
suspension
Japanese go
the $5 billio
construct. M
are expected
maintain th
infrastructu
roads, bridg
These facilit
entire econ
be too expe
individual o

POWER FOR ALL

If only one company produced something essential such as electricity, it could charge unreasonably high prices, and people would have no choice but to pay. To prevent this from happening, governments can either nationalize the industry (take it over), force the owners to charge fair prices, or pass laws to ensure that other companies can produce the same product, thus creating competition. In Germany, for example, private companies supply electricity but are tightly regulated by the government.

The Akashi-Kaikyo Bridge, Kobe, Japan, lit up at night

Measuring the economy

To FIND OUT HOW A COUNTRY'S ECONOMY is performing, it has to be measured. By comparing various economic measurements over time, governments can discover whether their policies are working, and if they need to be changed. One such measurement is gross domestic product (GDP), which is the value of all goods and services produced within a country in a year. However, it is difficult to compare the incomes of different-sized countries with this figure. GDP per capita is often used instead, since it measures the average GDP per person. This is calculated by dividing the country's GDP by its population. Other figures governments measure include inflation (the rate at which prices are rising), unemployment (the number of people without jobs), and education standards in schools. Governments also monitor and forecast their own expenditure from year to year.

1,463

1,116.3

796.2

604

09.8   506.8
    459.4

001 2002 2003 2004 2005 2006 2007
Year

H
that Brazil's GDP grew by almost
2000–07. Measuring a nation's
ows how much its economy is
ing. This helps governments to
estors to decide where to invest.
r everyone. Businesses thrive,
ues go up, and income and living
wever, rapid growth can cause
speculative bubbles that end in
e pages 36–39).

NATION
iam the Conqueror commissioned
land in England to figure out how
ould raise. The results were written down
ook, which listed the residents of 13,418
er with details of the land and property
veyor of the time
no single hide
nor indeed
w

Handwritten entry in the Domesday Book

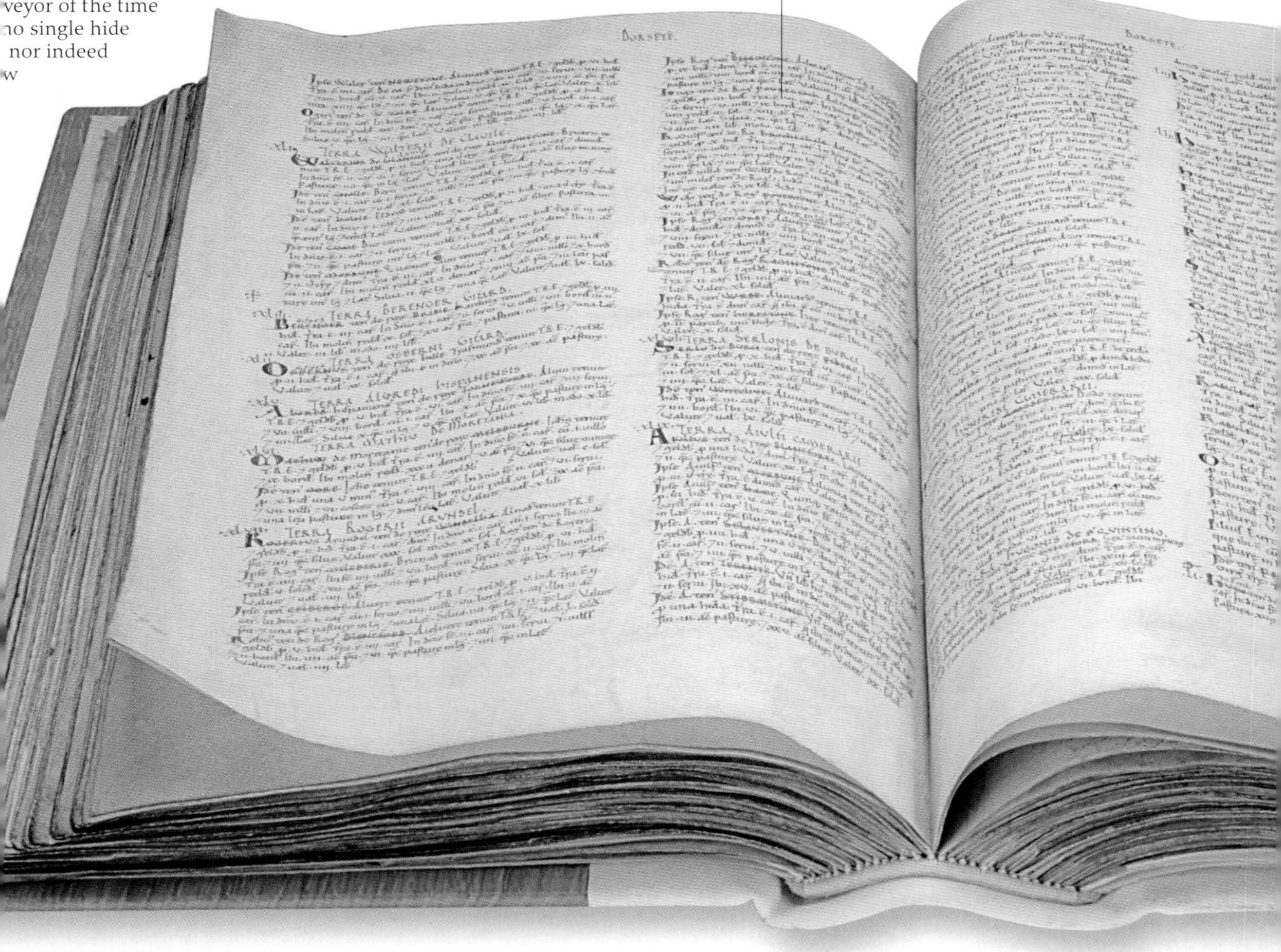

HOW HAPPY ARE YOU?
In 1972, King Jigme Singye Wangchuck of Bhutan proposed that the success of a nation should not be measured solely by economic growth or GDP, but by what he called gross national happiness, or GNH. It would take into account factors like the state of the environment and the preservation of cultural values. However, GNH is hard to measure and is not in widespread use.

Bhutanese children on their way to school

MEASURING DEVELOPMENT
The United Nations Development Program (UNDP) uses the Human Development Index, or HDI, to compare economies. Countries are graded in four categories: life expectancy (how long the average person can expect to live), GDP per person, adult literacy (the percentage of adults who can read), and the number of residents educated to primary, secondary, and college levels. Depending on their scores, the countries are then classified as developed, developing, or underdeveloped.

STANDING STILL
If an economy is neither growing nor shrinking, it is described as stagnating. How seriously this affects the economy depends on the overall state it is in when it stops growing. The Japanese economy has been stagnant in recent years, notably in the electronics industry, but Japan remains a prosperous country.

A Nepali girl carrying her baby brother

WORK WITHOUT PAY
Childcare and domestic chores such as cooking, cleaning, and washing clothes are often unpaid and not included in employment statistics. Globally, women perform a disproportionate amount of this "invisible work," sometimes in addition to paid jobs. The United Nations Development Program calculated that 70 percent of work done by women is unpaid, and valued it at $11 trillion a year.

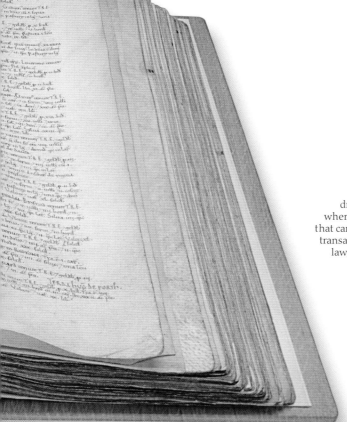

THE ILLEGAL ECONOMY
Criminal business activities such as selling drugs or fake goods and gambling (in places where it is illegal) are parts of the economy that cannot be accurately measured. These transactions take place outside of the law, so governments are unable to charge taxes on them.

A roulette wheel used in illegal gambling

Tax

GOVERNMENTS FINANCE THEIR ACTIVITIES by collecting taxes from individuals and businesses. Some taxes are collected directly. Income tax, for example, is charged as a percentage of a person's earnings. Other taxes, such as sales tax, are indirect, which means that people pay them only when they buy certain goods. This may influence the decisions people make about what to buy. When governments reduce taxes, people have more money to spend. This helps businesses to sell more, which has a positive effect on the economy. When governments increase taxes, to raise money to build new schools and hospitals, for example, people have less to spend. However, these government investments hopefully benefit the economy in the long term.

Energy-efficient bulb

A LIGHTER BURDEN
Tax charged on goods sold is known as sales tax. Governments can use taxation of goods to encourage or discourage certain activities. Tobacco and alcohol are often heavily taxed to discourage people from buying them. Meanwhile, products like eco-friendly light bulbs may be tax free to encourage their use.

PROGRESSIVE TAXES
If a tax is progressive, people with high incomes pay a larger percentage of their income than those making less. German political philosopher Karl Marx (1818–83) argued in favor of progressive taxes. He believed that by taxing the rich more than the poor, the amount of wealth in the economy would be distributed more fairly among the people.

PUTTING UP A FRONT
Sometimes, taxes have an undesired influence on human behavior. When the Dutch government imposed property tax based on the size of the fronts of houses in the Netherlands in the 17th century, people began building very narrow, deep houses. Similarly, in 1696, when the British government introduced a tax based on the number of windows each house had, people simply bricked up some of their windows.

Union Army uniform and rifle

THE PRICE OF WAR
In most countries the biggest source of government revenue is income tax, which is charged on a person's earnings. During the Civil War (1861–65), the government of the Northern states (the Union) introduced the United States' first income tax to fund troops and weapons in the fight against the Confederate Southern states.

REGRESSIVE TAXES

Some taxes are known as regressive, which means that the poor pay a higher proportion of their incomes than the rich. In 1989, the UK government introduced a poll tax that forced everyone in a particular area to pay the same amount, regardless of how wealthy they were. This was so unpopular that there were riots, and the government had to withdraw the tax.

Poster protesting against poll tax

SAFE HARBOR

Monte Carlo, a seaside resort in the tiny country of Monaco, is a popular destination for the rich and famous. So-called "tax havens" such as Monaco attract people because of their low or nonexistent taxes. Monaco offers tax benefits to its residents, so people buy expensive property here, and spend money on shopping and gambling at the casinos, bringing in revenue for the local economy. If governments set their taxes too high, people may move their businesses to such tax havens.

TAX ON LUXURY

Governments may claim that taxes on luxury goods, such as jewelry, are fair and progressive because no one is forced to buy these goods, and the rich are taxed more than the poor. Unless the taxes are carefully created, however, they may hurt the industries making the luxury goods, including the less wealthy workers. Also, what is considered a luxury can change. In Norway, a tax on chocolate introduced in 1922 continues to be charged, although chocolate is no longer a luxury item.

Narrow house in Amsterdam, the Netherlands

Inflation

INFLATION MEANS A RISE IN PRICES—not just the price of one item, but the prices of goods and services across a whole economy. Prices are set by supply and demand. If people have more money to spend on goods but not enough goods can be produced or imported to meet the extra demand, then prices rise. The result is inflation. If people choose to save more money and spend less, stores are left with large stocks of goods to sell, so prices fall. This is deflation. Inflation may also be affected by the prices of key commodities, such as oil, and the amount of money printed and circulated by government-controlled central banks. The rate of inflation is given as a percentage—an annual rate of 2 percent means that goods cost 2 percent more than they did a year ago. Both high inflation and deflation can disrupt the efficient workings of the economy.

BASKET OF GOODS
To see how prices are changing across a whole economy, and how that impacts on people's budgets, economists look at the changing price of a "basket of goods." This is a selection of goods that an average household buys. In different countries and at different times, the contents of the basket will change. In poorer countries, food, drink, and rent make up most of the basket. As societies become richer, more expensive consumer items, such as electronics and vacation travel, are also included.

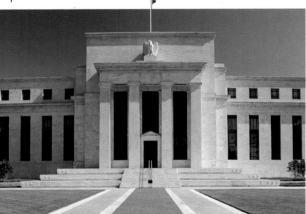

US Federal Reserve in Washington, DC

FIGHTING INFLATION
Governments put their central banks, such as the US Federal Reserve, in charge of money supply. Central banks try to keep inflation at a level that is neither too high nor too low so that prices remain stable. To do this, they can raise or lower interest rates (how much it costs to borrow money). If there is deflation, for example, lowering the interest rates encourages people to borrow money and spend more.

An elderly Russian woman receives a free hot meal in winter

HUMAN IMPACT
Not everyone is affected by inflation in the same way. Owners of assets with rising prices, such as houses, might benefit from inflation, while workers whose salaries rise in line with the rate of inflation will be no worse off. But inflation creates extra costs and uncertainties for businesses, since they must constantly update their prices and packaging, and can make only very short-term financial plans. The biggest losers are those on fixed incomes, especially retirees and people living off their savings. As inflation causes prices to rise, their fixed incomes buy less and less. In Russia during the 1990s, inflation caused great hardships for the nation's elderly, many of whom relied on tiny, fixed pensions from the state.

HYPERINFLATION

When inflation spirals out of control, it is called hyperinflation. In 1923, the German government printed huge quantities of money to pay off its debts. Prices doubled every two days, and savings became worthless. Money lost its value so fast that old money was used to light fires and as wallpaper! A new currency was introduced, and the economy finally stabilized in late 1923.

German children play with worthless Reichsmark notes in 1923

A line for gas in England during the oil crisis of the 1970s

OIL CRISIS

When companies have to pay more to manufacture or transport their products, they tend to compensate for their higher costs by raising the prices they charge consumers. In 1973, war in the Middle East disrupted global oil supplies. The price of oil quadrupled, fueling inflation in the oil-importing countries of the developed world. Since oil is not only vital for transportation but is also used in thousands of products and industrial processes, prices rose in every sector of the economy.

DEATH OF A CURRENCY

The worst hyperinflation of recent times occurred in Zimbabwe from 2004 to 2009. When the agricultural economy collapsed and tax revenues fell, Zimbabwe's central bank injected vast amounts of money into the economy. It was eventually printing bills as large as 100 trillion Zimbabwean dollars, as the monthly inflation rate reached more than 76 billion percent! The government abandoned the Zimbabwean dollar in 2009, allowing people to trade with the US dollar and the South African rand until a new currency could be launched.

Paying for fruit with 500,000 billion Zimbabwean dollars

The shadow economy

GANGSTER SHOOTOUTS, THRILLING CAR chases, pirates at sea, smugglers, and mafia wars—these are the stuff that popular movies are made of. Behind the excitement is a true story of criminal economic activity that makes up the shadow economy. This includes all the buying and selling that happens outside the law, such as the illegal manufacture and sale of drugs and alcohol, smuggling of banned goods, gambling, and selling of fake products. Pirated DVDs, software, and Internet downloads are also a part of the shadow economy. The scale of the problem is huge—the criminal activity in a poor country may be one-third as large in value as its legal economy. Governments all over the world want to get rid of this economy, because the goods and services offered are often dangerous and the cause of severe social problems. Also, criminals avoid paying taxes, resulting in a loss of revenue for the government.

YOUR MONEY OR YOUR LIFE
Between the 13th and 18th centuries, piracy (robbery at sea) was a widespread problem. Pirates with skull-and-crossbone flags may be a thing of the past, but piracy is still alive today, especially off the coast of Somalia, east Africa. Goods seized by pirates and sold illegally cause great loss to the economy.

GANGSTER BOSS
Al "Scarface" Capone was a famous criminal of the Prohibition era in the US. During the 1920s and early 1930s, the Chicago-based gangster controlled an illegal business empire worth around $100 million per year. The activities that brought in the most money were bootlegging and smuggling. Capone drove around in a bulletproof armored Cadillac, and called himself "just a businessman, giving the people what they want." He was finally imprisoned for not paying income tax.

DOWN THE DRAIN
In the 1920s, the US government passed a law banning the sale of alcohol in America. Known as Prohibition, this law sparked a wave of crime. Bootlegging—the making, selling, and transport of illegal alcohol—became highly profitable, and rival gangs battled for control of the trade. Respectable citizens rubbed shoulders with gangsters in "speakeasy" bars that were disguised as ice-cream parlours or hidden in basements. Liquor seized during police raids on these bars was often poured into sewers.

A GILDED LIFE
The Russian mafia consists of groups of criminals who control the illegal economy. Many of them adopt lavish lifestyles, owning luxury cars like this. Russia already had a thriving illegal economy when it was a communist country. At that time, banned goods such as jeans and electronic equipment were sold for huge profits. After the communist era ended in the early 1990s, there was widespread corruption due to lack of enforcement of regulations, and the mafia took advantage of this to amass wealth.

STRAPPED FOR CASH

Smugglers are people who bring goods into a country secretly. They do this either because the goods are illegal, or because they want to avoid paying import taxes on the goods. Smugglers go to great lengths to avoid detection. For instance, this man was caught at Los Angeles International Airport trying to smuggle rare birds into the US. Smuggling deprives the state of money it should receive in taxes on these goods.

Songbirds strapped to legs and concealed under pants

IN A FIX

Drugs made and sold illegally are a major cause of concern the world over. Users of these dangerous drugs often become addicted to them and may turn to crime to pay for their habit. Heroin, made from the seed pods of a certain type of poppy, commands a very high price on the illegal market. Drug smugglers often use their profits to finance other criminal activities.

A genuine Burberry bag, and a fake

SPOT THE FAKE

Branded goods such as watches, clothes, and handbags bearing the labels of famous companies are expensive. Customers pay because they trust the brands to deliver high quality. Some manufacturers sell counterfeit (fake) versions with the same labels at affordable prices. Buying these products is not illegal, but selling them is, as it damages the sales and reputation of the brand owners, such as Burberry. These labels are protected by law.

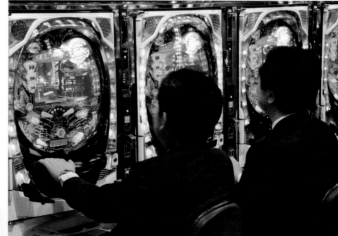

A DIFFERENT BALL GAME

Japanese law forbids gambling for money, so players of the popular pachinko pinball game instead receive prizes of electronic equipment and toys. There is usually a booth nearby where the prizes can be exchanged for cash. The owners of the booths then sell the prizes back to the pachinko parlor, and the business continues. These businesses, which are very profitable, are often run by the Yakuza (the Japanese mafia). Many people believe gambling activities like pachinko become an addiction and can ruin individuals and families financially.

A gold-plated Porsche

Unemployment

WHEN PEOPLE IN AN ECONOMY want work but cannot get any, they are said to be unemployed. Since paid work is the main form of livelihood for nearly everyone everywhere, unemployment can be a big problem for individuals, societies, and governments. Families face poverty, communities become divided, firms lose customers, and governments have big welfare bills to pay. Most economists agree that unemployment is caused by long-term changes in technology and production methods, short-term ups and downs of the national economy, and the impact of the wider global economy on local patterns of employment. Because long-term unemployment is so devastating, dealing with it is one of the main priorities of governments throughout the world.

Horse-drawn carriages share space with cars on a street in London, England, in 1912

THE PRICE OF CHANGE
Until about 1900, road traffic was pulled by horses, and the big cities of North America and Europe sustained a vast workforce of stable boys, riders, saddlers, and horse-feed merchants. But by 1930, the car had replaced the horse, and these jobs had almost vanished. Major technological advances like the invention of the automobile can render the workforce of an entire industry obsolete, and its workers' industry-specific skills worthless.

BEHIND THE TIMES
These saris from India are produced by traditional handicraft methods. Compared to factory-made saris, their production takes more time and people, and they are more expensive. Many Indian textile workers lost their livelihoods in the 19th and early 20th centuries when the country was flooded with cheap, machine-made textiles imported from Britain.

A FREE MEAL
Without a job, people may lose their homes and struggle to find enough money for food. All societies make provision to support the unemployed. In western European countries, the state takes care of the unemployed. In some other countries, charities and religious institutions such as churches and temples provide people with small donations, food, and shelter.

JOBS ON THE MOVE
Many jobs that were previously done in the developed world, such as telephone banking services, are increasingly done by workers in developing countries for lower wages. India has many call centers like the one above, that provide services such as ticket booking and customer help desks for global airlines. Call center workers in the developed world may be forced to find different work.

IN SEARCH OF A NEW LIFE
One way in which people respond to unemployment is to move to new places—even other countries—in search of work. In the 19th and early 20th centuries, millions of Europeans migrated to the rapidly expanding economies of the Americas in the hope of finding jobs and prosperity. In the early 21st century there is a new wave of economic migration, with many workers from poorer countries seeking a better livelihood in the nations of the developed world.

Immigrants from Europe arrive in New York City, 1892

CREATING EMPLOYMENT
Governments tackle unemployment in a number of ways. Workers made jobless by changes in technology are trained in new skills that make them more employable. The state may also try to create jobs itself, employing people in community-based programs such as planting trees. In Japan, the government invests in huge infrastructure projects, such as building roads and bridges, to keep employment in the construction sector high. Some argue that projects like these are too costly and spoil the appearance of the countryside.

Construction workers on an infrastructure project in the Shikoku region of Japan

Providing food for the unemployed in New Jersey

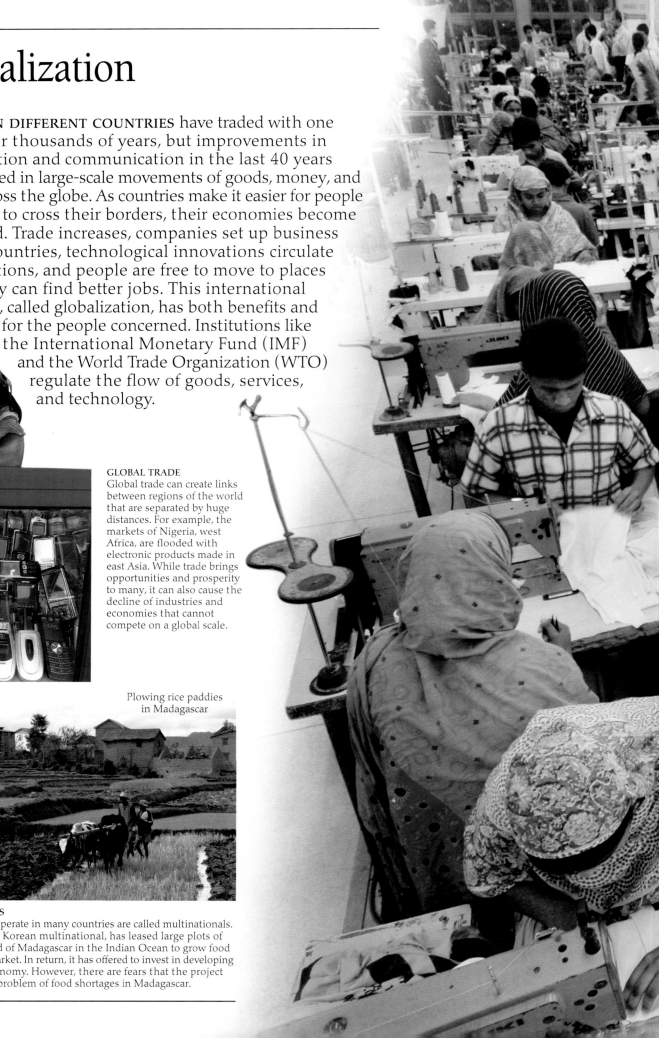

Globalization

PEOPLE IN DIFFERENT COUNTRIES have traded with one another for thousands of years, but improvements in transportation and communication in the last 40 years have resulted in large-scale movements of goods, money, and people across the globe. As countries make it easier for people and goods to cross their borders, their economies become interlinked. Trade increases, companies set up business in other countries, technological innovations circulate among nations, and people are free to move to places where they can find better jobs. This international movement, called globalization, has both benefits and drawbacks for the people concerned. Institutions like the International Monetary Fund (IMF) and the World Trade Organization (WTO) regulate the flow of goods, services, and technology.

GLOBAL TRADE
Global trade can create links between regions of the world that are separated by huge distances. For example, the markets of Nigeria, west Africa, are flooded with electronic products made in east Asia. While trade brings opportunities and prosperity to many, it can also cause the decline of industries and economies that cannot compete on a global scale.

Plowing rice paddies in Madagascar

MULTINATIONALS
Companies that operate in many countries are called multinationals. Daewoo, a South Korean multinational, has leased large plots of land on the island of Madagascar in the Indian Ocean to grow food for the Korean market. In return, it has offered to invest in developing Madagascar's economy. However, there are fears that the project will increase the problem of food shortages in Madagascar.

LOWER COSTS, HIGHER PROFITS
In a global economy, companies can locate different parts of their business in different areas of the world. In the global clothing industry, design, marketing, and most of the profits stay in the developed world, but the clothes are usually made in factories in developing countries, like this one in Bangladesh, where labor is cheap.
Some people say this system is unfair to the workers, since they work long hours for low wages. But the companies claim they are creating employment, which benefits the local economy.

DEVELOPMENT AND GLOBALIZATION
A global economy needs global organizers and regulators. The WTO sets rules for trading and settles disputes between nations. At the 2009 Aid for Trade conference in Geneva, Switzerland, Pascal Lamy, the director-general of the WTO, declared that global trade was the best way for poorer nations to develop.
Antiglobalization groups disagree, pointing out that powerful governments can impose trade restrictions that actually keep poor countries poor. The WTO's task is to address this problem.

MOBILE WORKFORCE
Cheap international transportation has made it easier for people to travel far afield in search of jobs. This Indian construction worker, for example, has found employment in Dubai in the Middle East. A mobile labor force also benefits employers. Large companies often scour the globe to recruit the very best engineers, designers, scientists, IT experts, and managers the world has to offer.

WINNERS AND LOSERS
This portable computer hard drive is just one of the many products developed in Silicon Valley in California. With the worldwide computer and Internet boom of the late 1990s, high-tech areas like Silicon Valley became prosperous almost overnight. In contrast, the car industry in Michigan has been badly hit by fierce global competition in recent years.

Rich and poor

SINCE HUMAN BEINGS began abandoning nomadic and hunter-gatherer lifestyles for farming and settling in villages and cities 10,000 years ago, economic output has soared. But this output and the wealth it creates have never been evenly divided. In the modern world, there is a vast gulf between rich and poor nations, and inequalities of income within societies seem to be growing. Inequality and poverty are among the most important global issues, and not just for moral and political reasons—they also affect the economy itself. Populations that are too poor to consume provide no market for businesses, and social groups that are too poor to educate themselves provide a small pool of skilled labor. Inequality also hampers economic development—unequal societies are unstable and liable to be divided by conflict.

TOO POOR TO TAKE PART
Some definitions of poverty involve asking whether a person has the resources to join in with mainstream society. In developed countries, surveys of the public suggest that people feel owning a TV, a cell phone, and a suit are the minimum needed to take part in the community. In the developing world, this would place someone far above the poverty line.

INEQUALITY WITHIN SOCIETIES
This view of São Paulo, the richest city in Brazil, shows the huge economic inequalities that can exist within a society. In the foreground is a shanty town of temporary dwellings, while the apartment blocks of the wealthy tower in the distance. Increasingly, the cities of the developing world are marked by walls, armed guards, and fortresslike architecture that separate the rich from the poor.

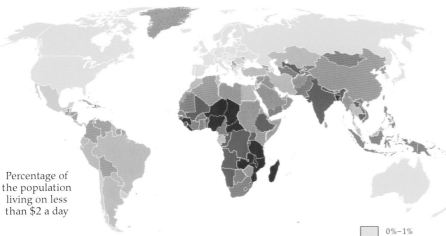

Percentage of the population living on less than $2 a day

	0%–1%
	2%–5%
	6%–20%
	21%–40%
	41%–60%
	61%–80%
	81%–100%
	No data

INEQUALITY BETWEEN COUNTRIES
The World Bank considers that the baseline of absolute poverty (the minimum income required to survive) is $2 a day. More than 2.5 billion people live around or below this level of income. This map shows that the world's poorest people are concentrated in the developing world, especially in sub-Saharan Africa and south Asia, and they are almost entirely absent from Europe, North America, and east Asia. Significant numbers of very poor people remain in the rural areas of Indonesia, China, and Brazil.

STAYING RICH

The British private school system is a good example of how the rich hold on to their money. The financial wealth of one generation is invested in the elite education of the next generation, such as these pupils from Eton College. Their expensive schooling equips them with highly valued academic skills and cultural knowledge, and connections to some of the most wealthy and influential people in society. These, in turn, help the graduates of the private school system to occupy the top jobs and command the highest incomes.

Chair lift makes a bus more accessible to a wheelchair user

DEALING WITH INEQUALITY

Income is divided unequally between different social groups, between men and women, and between people of different ethnic origins. Those with disabilities are further challenged by a lack of job opportunities and difficulty in accessing transportation and workplaces. Governments try to redress these inequalities by passing laws protecting employees' rights. But a fair society costs money. For example, powered wheelchairs and ramps on public transportation are a boon to disabled people in rich countries, but their high cost makes them rare in the developing world.

Can aid work?

Aɪᴅ ɪꜱ ᴛʜᴇ ᴛʀᴀɴꜱꜰᴇʀ ᴏꜰ ᴡᴇᴀʟᴛʜ from rich to poor nations in order to promote economic development. However, the record of aid in stimulating growth and reducing poverty is very mixed. Some experts argue that increasing exports to richer nations is a better way of helping developing countries out of poverty, but this too has its limits. New solutions are emerging, with consumers in the developed world backing fair trade programs that guarantee fair prices for poor farmers, and the governments of rich countries canceling the debts of poor nations. In the developing world, micro-credit programs are helping some of the poorest people to set up businesses, while cell phones are empowering communities by linking them to the wider world.

AID THAT WORKS
Developing nations are short of infrastructure (facilities), technology, and finance, and overwhelmed by the needs of their growing populations for basic services, such as water supply. Aid can help to build sewage plants and provide clean water. However, for aid to be truly effective, local people also need to be trained to maintain these facilities in the long term.

Tank carries public-health information

A USEFUL SPINOFF
Aid works best when it is used to fund long-term projects, rather than being used as a short-term "fix." Projects that promote education, health, and self-sufficiency are most likely to produce lasting results. These South African children are having fun turning a merry-go-round that doubles as a water pump. There are now more than 1,000 of these innovative PlayPumps in sub-Saharan Africa, providing clean drinking water to more than 1 million impoverished people. The spinning motion provided by the children pumps underground water into a large storage tank raised above the ground. The tank carries advertising, which provides funds for the upkeep of the pump, and public-health messages.

LOANS FOR THE POOR
Micro-credit programs lend very small amounts of money (micro-loans) to help those in poverty set up businesses. Marium Begum runs her own poultry farm in Bangladesh. She began the business with a micro-loan from the Grameen Bank, which provides financial services for the poor. As the businesses repay their loans, the bank uses the money to fund new projects.

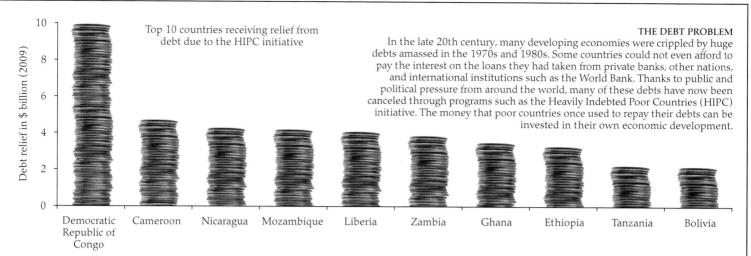

Top 10 countries receiving relief from debt due to the HIPC initiative

Debt relief in $ billion (2009)

Democratic Republic of Congo · Cameroon · Nicaragua · Mozambique · Liberia · Zambia · Ghana · Ethiopia · Tanzania · Bolivia

THE DEBT PROBLEM
In the late 20th century, many developing economies were crippled by huge debts amassed in the 1970s and 1980s. Some countries could not even afford to pay the interest on the loans they had taken from private banks, other nations, and international institutions such as the World Bank. Thanks to public and political pressure from around the world, many of these debts have now been canceled through programs such as the Heavily Indebted Poor Countries (HIPC) initiative. The money that poor countries once used to repay their debts can be invested in their own economic development.

FAIR TRADE
The fair trade movement aims to guarantee high and stable prices for poor farmers in the developing world, so that they do not have to rely on the low, erratic prices of conventional markets. This ethical approach is supported by many consumers in richer nations, who are happy to pay higher prices knowing that the farmers get a fairer deal. Spurred on by customer demand, supermarket chains are increasingly adopting fairly traded products, especially tea, coffee, chocolate, and fruit such as bananas.

Fairly traded coffee beans

TRADE, NOT AID
Growth through exports to rich nations is often hindered by trade regulations. For many years, the US banned shrimp imports from Malaysia and Thailand on the grounds that they did not meet its tough environmental standards, since sea turtles often became caught in the shrimp nets. The shrimp exporters argued that this was putting the interests of turtles before the welfare of the poor. The ban was ruled illegal by the World Trade Organization.

Turning the merry-go-round drives a water pump

Cell phone keeps this Maasai herder in touch with cattle prices

IN TOUCH WITH THE WORLD
Poor nations can fall even further behind rich nations unless they find ways to adopt the latest technologies. Fortunately, cell phone networks are less costly to construct than conventional telephone lines. There were just 1 million cell phone subscribers in Africa in 1996. Ten years later, there were 215 million, and Africa's demand for phones continues to grow. This Kenyan Maasai herder can use his cell phone to receive information about local and national cattle markets so that he can get the best prices for his livestock.

Future challenges

THE ECONOMIC HISTORY OF the 21st century will be every bit as tumultuous as that of the 20th century. The challenges facing the global economy are dominated by a rapid rise in the world's population. At the same time, the standard of living has increased in the developing world. A greater number of wealthier people everywhere will consume vastly more goods and resources. As consumption rises, pollution goes up, worsening the increasing environmental problems of climate change, and energy and water shortages. There will be no single solution to all of these problems. We will need to find new ways to prevent pollution and encourage consumers to favor being thrifty rather than wasteful.

POPULATION EXPLOSION
This crowded street is in the Chinese city of Guangzhou, whose population has grown from less than 1 million people to more than 12 million in a few decades. Like the global population, Guangzhou will continue to grow for the next 40 years. The United Nations predicts that the world's population will peak at around 9.5 billion in 2050. Most of these people will live in cities in the developing world. To sustain such vast numbers, the global economy will have to use Earth's limited resources far more efficiently.

Ears of wheat

FOOD SHORTAGE
A changing climate, growing population, and rising living standards may strain the global food supply. Wheat prices soared in 2005–06 due to a decline in harvests caused by severe drought and growing consumer demand for wheat. In the future, diets in the developing world may change from vegetables and rice or wheat to include more meat. It takes far more land and water to produce meat, putting further pressure on the Earth's resources.

Chimney allows fumes from furnace to escape _____

OIL-FREE ECONOMICS
The global economy is driven by oil. In addition to keeping our transportation going, oil is burned to generate electricity, and it is a raw material from which we make many key substances. But our oil reserves cannot meet rising demand forever. The transition to a global economy that is not oil dependent will not be easy. Whole industries will disappear, but others will emerge as new, oil-free technologies are developed.

Gas, derived from oil, fuels the world's cars

Gasoline pump nozzle

WATER WARS
This cracked, parched earth of Australia was once rich, fertile farmland. Freshwater resources are limited and overexploited throughout the world. While drought has diminished the supply, rising populations, water-hungry manufacturing processes, and excessive irrigation (watering of farmland) have driven up demand. In some parts of the world, the struggle for water resources may become so fierce that military conflicts could break out between nations.

CLIMATE CHANGE
Emissions of carbon dioxide and other polluting gases from burning fossil fuels (coal, oil, and gas) have caused a steady rise in global temperatures and an increase in extreme weather. Faced with the dangers of global climate change, governments are introducing programs, often called green taxes, to charge for emissions from cars, factories, and power plants. Due to green taxes, electricity from this coal-fired plant will become more expensive, while electricity generated by wind and solar power, and other forms of renewable energy, will get cheaper. This should cause people to switch from "dirty" sources of power to environmentally friendly sources.

AN AGING WORLD
The population of the developed world is aging fast as the birth rate falls and individuals live longer. How will a declining workforce support growing numbers of elderly people who require care? The ways in which we save, organize our retirement, look after our families, and plan our working lives will have to change to accommodate this dramatic shift in the makeup of the global population.

The economy and you

EVERY PERSON ON THE PLANET is part of the economy. The economic wealth of the nation you live in, and how the government decides to raise and spend taxes, can determine something as basic as whether you have access to clean drinking water. It influences the facilities available in your local school, what health care you receive, the price of food and clothing, and the types of industry and business that develop in your area. Your family's income may decide what size your home is, which neighborhood you live in, what school you go to, and where you spend your vacations. All governments, businesses, and individuals—including you—budget by planning how to spend or save money. That is the key to a well-run economy—making the best possible use of limited resources.

A SCHOOL LIKE MINE
Everything about your school, from the equipment and facilities to the number of pupils per teacher, depends on economic factors. Some schools are funded through taxes, others through tuition paid by parents. Students in well-funded schools can enjoy access to the latest technology, while classrooms in less-privileged regions may be overcrowded and lack even basic equipment.

FUTURE PLANNING
People have saved spare change in money boxes, such as this modern piggy bank, since ancient Greek times, more than 2,000 years ago. Saving money to buy something expensive at a later date is an example of how individuals make economic plans, or budgets—just as governments and companies do, but on a smaller scale.

CITY LIVING

The economic wealth of the area you grow up in can have a huge effect on the opportunities available to you in life. More than half the world's population now lives in cities, compared to just 9 percent in 1900. One of the main reasons why people move from the countryside to towns is to find work or improve financial prospects. Tokyo, Japan, is one of the largest and richest cities in the world. The headquarters of many international corporations are located there, and the 12.8 million Tokyo residents commute to jobs in stores, factories, offices, and hospitals. Someone living in a rural area with limited transportation options may not have the same employment opportunities.

STARTING TOO YOUNG

These Iraqi girls are paid to collect garbage and carry it to the local dump. They are among an estimated 158 million children aged 5–14 worldwide who have to work for a living. Often their jobs are dangerous, they are always badly paid, and those who work full time miss out on education. But many poor families depend on the money their children earn.

CROWDED HOMES

The kind of house you live in is determined by economic factors such as the wealth of your family and house prices in your neighborhood. This family can afford to live only in a small one-room hut in a slum area of Yangon, the capital city of Myanmar (Burma). The hut is overcrowded, and there is no running water, electricity, or facility for sewage collection. The family members are at risk of developing serious health problems, including diseases such as cholera and dysentery.

BURGERNOMICS

In 2006, the Swiss bank UBS came up with an interesting way of comparing economic conditions in different cities. It calculated how much time a person earning the average wage of a city worker needed to work to be able to buy a Big Mac from a local branch of multinational food chain McDonald's. The results varied from 10 minutes in Tokyo, Japan, to 97 minutes in Bogota, Colombia.

World in numbers

THE NUMBERS NEEDED to describe the global economy just keep on rising. In 1900, the total value of goods and services produced by all the countries in the world was $1 trillion (million million). It has since multiplied almost 70 times. Today's global economy has more trade, billionaires, and multinational corporations than ever before. Recently, there has also been a notable shift in the balance of economic power toward developing nations, such as China and India.

United States
359 billionaires in 2009

Nonfinancial assets ($290 trillion)
These include land, property, shares, bonds, and any items of value other than money. The value the world placed on its assets peaked at this level in late 2008.

Traditional banking ($39 trillion)
This is all the money held in bank deposits and savings accounts around the world, plus all the money individuals and businesses have borrowed from banks.

Cash in circulation ($3.9 trillion)
This is the value of all the currency in the world, but does not include money traded electronically. If everyone emptied their bank accounts and sold their financial assets, there would not be enough cash to pay everyone.

Gold reserves ($845 billion)
Although the world now runs on a system of fiat money (a currency has value because a government says it does), central banks still maintain deposits of gold in case of emergency. They are small compared to the amount of cash in the world.

HOW MUCH MONEY IS THERE IN THE WORLD?

The total amount of cash in the world is only a small fraction of the virtual money being traded by people in the finance industry, as these figures from 2008 show. Compare these figures with the global GDP (gross domestic product)—the value of all the goods and services produced on the planet in a year, which in 2008 was valued at $69.49 trillion.

GLOBAL GIANTS

This graph shows how much the major regions of the world have contributed to the world economy since the year 1500. Back then, India and China were the economic superpowers, although western Europe was just beginning to challenge them. The Americas contributed less than 5 percent of global GDP at that time. From the beginning of the 19th century, the balance of global GDP shifted decisively as a result of the industrial revolutions in Europe and North America (see page 66). By 1950, the United States alone accounted for 30 percent of global GDP, and western Europe and Japan another 30 percent. While the developed countries still account for a majority of world output, developing countries are on the rise.

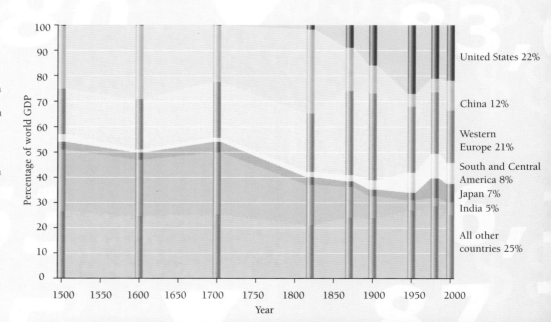

United States 22%

China 12%

Western Europe 21%

South and Central America 8%

Japan 7%

India 5%

All other countries 25%

Percentage of world GDP — Year

Germany
54

China
47

Russia
32

United Kingdom
25

India
24

Canada
20

Japan
17

Brazil
13

Turkey
13

Saudi Arabia
13

Spain
12

COUNTRIES WITH THE MOST BILLIONAIRES

The growing global economy has made it possible for some people to make gigantic fortunes. The number of billionaires (in US dollars) continues to rise, as industrial and banking tycoons from Europe and North America are joined by oil and mining magnates from Russia and Saudi Arabia. In the last 20 years, the computer industry has swollen the ranks of the US's band of billionaires.

RANK	COMPANY	2008 VALUE ($)
1	Google	66,434,000,000
2	General Electric	61,880,000,000
3	Microsoft	54,951,000,000
4	Coca-Cola	44,134,000,000
5	China Mobile	41,214,000,000
6	Marlboro	39,166,000,000
7	Wal-mart	36,880,000,000
8	Citi	33,706,000,000
9	IBM	33,572,000,000
10	Toyota	33,427,000,000
11	McDonald's	33,138,000,000
12	Nokia	31,670,000,000
13	Bank of America	28,767,000,000
14	BMW	25,751,000,000
15	HP	24,987,000,000
16	Apple	24,728,000,000
17	UPS	24,580,000,000
18	Wells Fargo	24,284,000,000
19	American Express	23,113,000,000
20	Louis Vuitton	22,686,000,000

MOST VALUABLE BRAND-NAME COMPANIES

In today's fearsomely competitive global markets, where companies are fighting to attract the attention of billions of consumers, a successful brand is among the most prized and valuable assets. Google is worth many billions on the stock market because it has become the world's most popular Internet search engine. This enables it to provide advertisers with a huge audience. Of course, a fantastic brand cannot be built on the back of a useless service or product. Many of the companies on this list were pioneers in their fields, such as IBM in computers and Nokia in mobile telephones.

GLOBAL EXPORTS

At the end of World War II, global trade was worth $59 billion. Since then, the growth of trade between nations has been explosive, reaching more than $13 trillion in 2007. The World Trade Organization (WTO) encourages nations to reduce high tariffs (taxes) on imports, making trade easier. Meanwhile, the invention of the Internet and cheaper transportation have reduced the costs of doing global business.

$13,619 billion

$7,375 billion

$3,675 billion

$1,838 billion

$579 billion

$157 billion

$84 billion

$59 billion

| 1948 | 1953 | 1963 | 1973 | 1983 | 1993 | 2003 | 2007 |

HIGHEST INCOME

The United States may have the highest GDP of any nation, but if that figure is divided by the number of people living in the US, it is no longer on top. In 2008, Norway had the highest income per capita (GDP divided by population).

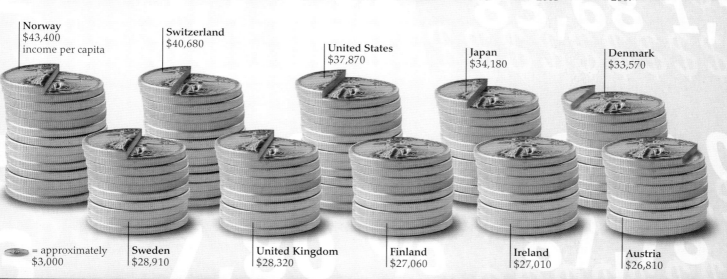

Norway
$43,400
income per capita

Switzerland
$40,680

United States
$37,870

Japan
$34,180

Denmark
$33,570

= approximately $3,000

Sweden
$28,910

United Kingdom
$28,320

Finland
$27,060

Ireland
$27,010

Austria
$26,810

Timeline

THE STORY OF THE WORLD ECONOMY over the last 12,000 years is dominated by people devising ingenious ways of getting the most out of limited resources such as time, land, and people. Some of the most important innovations, such as the railroad and the Internet, have been technological, while others have involved the creation of institutions such as banks and stock markets.

A postcard showing the Boston Tea Party, in the American colony of Massachusetts, 1773

c. 10,000–6000 BCE EMERGENCE OF FARMING
The development of farming spells the end of the old hunter-gatherer lifestyle in many parts of the world.

c. 7500–4000 BCE FIRST TOWNS
The world's first towns develop. A new kind of urban-based economy is formed with the growth of settlements such as Çatalhöyük in southern Turkey.

Mesopotamian clay tablet with accounts written in cuneiform script, c. 2750 BCE

c. 3400–2700 BCE EARLY ACCOUNTANTS
People in Mesopotamia develop a method of writing called cuneiform to keep records, or accounts, of trading and banking transactions.

c. 1200 BCE CHINESE COWRIE MONEY
The Chinese start using cowrie-shell money. Cowries were still being used as money in parts of Africa as recently as the mid-20th century.

c. 640 BCE FIRST COINS
The world's first true coins are minted in Lydia, a part of modern-day Turkey.

c. 490 BCE FIRST NAMED BANKER
The financial dealings of a Lydian banker named Pythius are documented by Herodotus, a Greek historian.

30 BCE–14 CE REIGN OF AUGUSTUS
Emperor Augustus transforms the Roman Empire, issuing new coins and introducing new taxes on sales, land, and individuals.

306–337 CE CONSTANTINE'S COIN
Roman Emperor Constantine issues a gold coin, the solidus, that will continue to be produced for 700 years.

806–821 PAPER MONEY
Paper money originates with the world's first banknotes issued in China.

1156 FOREIGN-CURRENCY EXCHANGE
Two brothers borrow 115 Genoese pounds from an Italian bank. They agree to repay the loan as 460 bezants (a different currency) to the bank's agents in Constantinople, thus starting the earliest foreign exchange contract.

1288 FIRST SHARE CERTIFICATE
A letter is sent to a Swedish company confirming the sale of one-eighth of the Stora copper mining company. This document proving share ownership is the first share certificate.

1346–50 BLACK DEATH
A deadly plague reduces Europe's population by more than a third, dramatically improving the surviving workers' bargaining power for pay.

1403 ITALIAN BANKING TAKES OFF
Interest charges are legalized in Florence, paving the way for a banking explosion.

Spanish coins made from gold and silver taken from Native Americans, 16th century

1492 EUROPEANS DISCOVER THE AMERICAS
Christopher Columbus's discovery of the Americas begins a dramatic expansion of the global economy.

1498 SEA TRADE BETWEEN EUROPE AND ASIA
Vasco da Gama's discovery of a sea route to India opens up big new markets for both Europeans and Asians.

c. 1500–40 SPANISH GOLD
Spanish conquistadors conquer the Aztecs of Mexico and the Incas of Peru and plunder their gold. So much gold is sent back to Europe that the price of gold goes down.

1502 SLAVE TRADE BEGINS
The first African slaves reach the Americas. Over the next 300 years, more than 12 million African slaves are shipped to the Americas to work unpaid on plantations and in mines.

1634–37 TULIP MANIA
In the Netherlands, demand for rare varieties of tulips makes tulip prices skyrocket, creating a giant speculative bubble.

c. 1750 INDUSTRIAL REVOLUTION BEGINS
New manufacturing techniques based on water- and steam-powered machinery are introduced in Britain, marking the beginning of the Industrial Revolution.

1773 BOSTON TEA PARTY
American colonists dressed as Native Americans protest against British import taxes by throwing a ship's cargo of tea into Boston harbor. The protest sets America on a path to independence.

1776 THE WEALTH OF NATIONS
Adam Smith publishes his influential book on economics, *An Inquiry into the Nature and Causes of the Wealth of Nations*.

1799 INCOME TAX
British Prime Minister William Pitt introduces income tax, a tax based on personal income, to fund the war against French leader Napoleon.

1804–29 STEAM RAILROADS
Richard Trevithick demonstrates the first steam-driven railroad engine in Merthyr Tydfil, Wales. By 1829, commercial railroads are in use between Stockton and Darlington and between Liverpool and Manchester, England.

1807 BRITAIN OUTLAWS THE SLAVE TRADE
The slave trade is abolished in the British Empire, and the Royal Navy enforces an international ban on the trade. The US outlaws slavery in 1863.

1838 INSTANT MESSAGES
The invention of the electric telegraph allows messages to be sent rapidly over long distances.

1854 JAPAN OPENS ITS DOORS
After more than 200 years of isolation, Japan opens its ports to foreign trade.

1856 STEEL REVOLUTION
The Bessemer process of converting iron to steel is invented, improving the output of the world's metal industries.

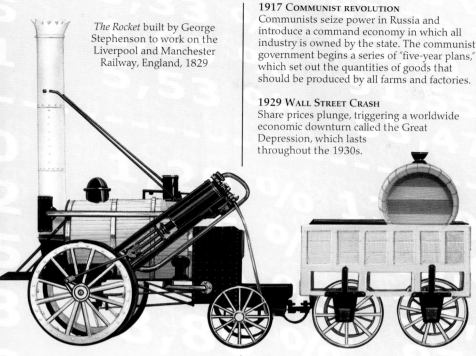

The Rocket built by George Stephenson to work on the Liverpool and Manchester Railway, England, 1829

1917 COMMUNIST REVOLUTION
Communists seize power in Russia and introduce a command economy in which all industry is owned by the state. The communist government begins a series of "five-year plans," which set out the quantities of goods that should be produced by all farms and factories.

1929 WALL STREET CRASH
Share prices plunge, triggering a worldwide economic downturn called the Great Depression, which lasts throughout the 1930s.

1978 CHINA ALLOWS PRIVATE ENTERPRISE
China's communist government allows farmers to sell what they grow for cash they can keep. They no longer have to work on farms owned by the government.

1979 FIRST MOBILE PHONE NETWORK
Japanese firm NTT establishes the first commercial mobile telephone network.

1980s REAGANOMICS
US President Ronald Reagan introduces a program of tax cuts, reduced government spending, and reduced regulation of businesses to boost the American economy.

1989 WORLD WIDE WEB
English computer scientist Tim Berners-Lee proposes a system that later evolves into the World Wide Web, eventually giving hundreds of millions of people new access to markets.

1989 BERLIN WALL FALLS
The fall of the Berlin Wall dividing East and West Berlin marks the collapse of communism and the reunification of Germany. In 1989–91, communist governments lose power throughout eastern Europe and Russia.

1857 BANKING CRISIS
In October, financial panic forces 1,415 US banks to suspend customer withdrawals of gold and silver, triggering recession on both sides of the Atlantic.

1869 SUEZ CANAL
The opening of the Suez Canal connects the Mediterranean and Red seas, drastically reducing sailing times between Europe and Asia.

1944 BRETTON WOODS AGREEMENT
Representatives of 44 countries sign an agreement on rebuilding the world financial system after World War II. They agree on a method of fixed currency exchange rates and create the International Monetary Fund (IMF).

1945–60 POSTWAR CONSUMER BOOM
The world economy recovers quickly after World War II, and newly affluent consumers buy modern, luxury products such as televisions, refrigerators, and automobiles.

1957 EUROPEAN UNITY
Six European nations agree to abolish trade barriers between one another, forming an economic alliance that will grow into the European Union.

1973 OIL CRISIS
Several oil-producing nations suspend supply to the US and Europe, causing oil prices to quadruple and inflation to rise.

1991 INDIAN REFORMS
The Indian government passes laws encouraging firms to compete with one another and foreign companies, leading to a period of rapid growth.

2000 DOTCOM CRASH
A speculative bubble in shares of Internet companies bursts dramatically, leading to disastrous drops in share prices.

2008 CREDIT CRUNCH
The world is plunged into recession by a financial crisis caused by high-risk lending.

Poster of Joseph Stalin introducing a five-year plan to the people of Russia, 1946

1874 TELEPHONE
Alexander Graham Bell invents the telephone. This technological innovation opens up a world of new business possibilities.

1908–13 ASSEMBLY LINE
Henry Ford invents the assembly line and produces the world's first mass-produced, affordable car—the Model T Ford.

UXB 12

The 1950 Porsche 356, a car bought by well-off consumers during the postwar boom

Glossary

AGRICULTURE
The production of food through farming. It includes growing crops and raising animals and is one of the main sectors of the economy.

ASSET
An item owned by an individual or company that has value and can be used to generate wealth. Shares, land, and property are all examples of assets.

BALANCE OF TRADE
The value of a country's exports minus the value of its imports.

BANKRUPTCY
The state a person or business is in when deemed by law to be unable to pay their debts.

A modern combine harvester, an agricultural machine

BARTER
The exchange of goods and services for other goods and services without the use of money.

BOND
A certificate of debt issued by a company or a government in which the borrower promises to repay the money to the holder along with interest by a future date. Bonds are transferable, meaning that they can be bought and sold.

BOOM
A period of very rapid economic growth, often unsustainable and ending in a bust.

BUBBLE
A sudden rise in the price of an asset or group of assets to levels far above its true value.

BUST
The opposite of a boom, in which an economy experiences a sudden and dramatic downturn.

CAPITAL
"Real capital" is machines, factories, and other possessions used to produce goods and services. "Financial capital" is money that can be used to purchase real capital.

CAPITALISM
An economic system in which the means of production, distribution, and exchange are mostly privately owned.

CARTEL
A group of companies that work together to fix their prices higher than they would be if set within a competitive free market.

A bribe—a form of corruption

CENTRAL BANK
An organization in charge of regulating a nation's money supply.

COMMAND ECONOMY
An economic system in which key decisions about production and distribution are made by the government.

COMMISSION
A fee paid to the sellers of goods and services based on percentages of the total cost.

COMMODITY
A basic good such as grain or iron that is the same no matter who produces it—unlike goods such as televisions, which may vary in quality.

COMMUNISM
An economic system in which the means of production (factories, equipment, and raw materials) are owned and controlled by the state.

COMPETITION
A situation in which two or more companies vie to win the business of potential buyers by offering favorable terms.

CONSUMERISM
An economic theory that suggests an ever-increasing consumption is beneficial to the economy.

CONSUMPTION
The use of goods and services.

CORRUPTION
Abuse of power, such as a bribe in exchange for favors or influence.

CREDIT
Money available for an individual or business to borrow.

CREDIT CRUNCH
A sudden reduction in availability of loans from banks, making borrowing difficult and expensive. The 2008 global financial crisis involved a massive worldwide credit crunch.

CREDITOR
A person or business to whom money is owed.

CURRENCY
The form of money used within a particular country or group of countries. The dollar is the currency of the United States, the pound sterling is the currency in the United Kingdom, and the euro is the currency in 16 European nations.

DEBTOR
A person or business that owes money to a creditor.

An artist's impression of a debtor's prison

DEFAULT
Failure to pay money owed.

DEFLATION
A decrease in the overall level of the prices of goods and services in the economy. The opposite is inflation.

DEMAND
The quantity of a good or service that people are willing and able to buy at a particular price in a market.

Coffee beans produced by a fair-trade cooperative

DEMOCRACY
A political system in which power is held by the people through their elected representatives.

DEPOSIT
A sum of money placed with a bank. It can also mean a sum of money put down as part payment for a good or service, with the balance to be paid later.

DEPRESSION
A severe and prolonged downturn in economic activity of a nation or group of nations.

DERIVATIVES
Complex financial contracts that are based on the value of underlying assets such as shares, commodities, currencies, interest rates, and market indexes. Derivatives traded in exchange markets are settled for money, not by delivering the actual assets.

DEVELOPED COUNTRIES
Nations that have strong, technology-driven economies and whose citizens enjoy a high standard of living.

DEVELOPING COUNTRIES
Nations that have less technologically advanced economies and lower standards of living.

DICTATORSHIP
Rule of a country by one all-powerful individual.

DISTRIBUTION
The transport of finished products from factories to stores to consumers.

DIVIDENDS
Payments made by companies to their shareholders from after-tax profits.

DIVISION OF LABOR
The separation of work into tasks performed by different specialists to improve productivity.

ECONOMICS
The study of how wealth is created and distributed in a community.

ECONOMIES OF SCALE
Savings in production costs as a business grows larger—the more items produced, the less they cost on average to produce.

ECONOMY
The system of production, consumption, and distribution within a society.

EFFICIENCY
Getting the greatest possible output from limited resources, such as time and money.

EXCHANGE
A forum for buying and selling.

EXCHANGE RATE
The price of one currency in terms of another.

EXPORTS
Goods and services sold to other countries.

FAIR TRADE
A movement that aims to ensure that workers in developing countries are paid more than they would be if the prices of the goods they produce were left to ordinary market forces.

FEUDALISM
Medieval economic system in which landowners gave farmers parcels of land to work in return for a share of the produce and military service.

FINANCIAL DISTRICT
An area with a cluster of banks, stockbroker firms, and other financial institutions.

FISCAL
Relating to taxation and government spending.

FREE MARKET
Economic system in which prices are determined only by supply and demand.

Zecchini, gold coins first minted in Venice, 1284

FUTURES
Contracts to buy or sell assets at agreed upon dates in the future for prices determined in the present. A type of derivative.

GDP
Gross Domestic Product, or the value of all the goods and services produced within a country during one year.

GOLD STANDARD
An international system that fixed the values of the currency of participating nations in terms of specified quantities of gold. It is no longer used.

HYPERINFLATION
A period in which prices rise out of control, leaving a country's currency worthless.

IMPORTS
Goods and services purchased from people in another country.

INCOME
Money earned through employment and other investments.

INDEX
A single number calculated from a set of prices used to represent the value of something—for example, the top 100 shares traded on a stock market. Market analysts can monitor changes in an index.

INDUSTRY
People or companies involved in a particular sector of economic activity, such as agriculture, steel, paper, or music.

INFLATION
A rise in the prices of goods and services over a period of time.

INFRASTRUCTURE
The facilities and services needed to support economic activity and the functioning of a community, such as roads, bridges, water systems, and electric power.

INSURANCE
An arrangement whereby companies promise to pay their clients if particular events occur (for example, theft or fire). Insurance allows people to protect themselves against risk by making small, regular payments.

INTELLECTUAL PROPERTY
Ideas and inventions protected by law so that people cannot use them without the permission of their owners.

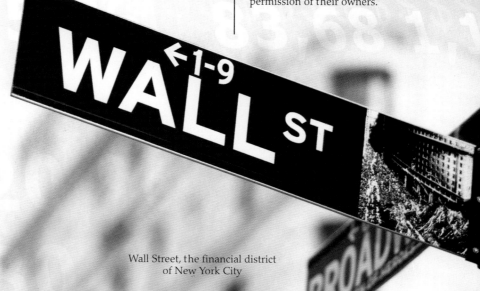

Wall Street, the financial district of New York City

INTEREST
Fees paid by borrowers to lenders, usually expressed as a percentage of the sum borrowed.

INTERNATIONAL MONETARY FUND
An interntional financial organization that makes loans to national governments when their economies are threatened by financial crises.

INVESTMENT
The purchase of an asset, such as machinery, in the hope of making a return, or profit.

LIMITED LIABILITY
A legal arrangement whereby a company's shareholders are not responsible for paying its debts beyond the value of the money they have put into the firm.

LIQUIDITY
The extent to which an asset can be easily converted into cash.

LOAN
A sum of money given to an individual or business that must be repaid later, often with added interest fees.

MANUFACTURING
One of the main sectors of the economy, it is the industrial use of tools and labor to make something.

MARKET
A place either physical or virtual in which people meet to trade.

MARKET FORCES
The supply and demand of goods and services.

MARXISM
A political theory from the writings of 19th-century German theorist Karl Marx. He argued that workers exploited by capitalism will rebel, bringing about communism.

MIGRATION
The movement of people from one country or region to another.

MINIMUM WAGE
The lowest wage that an employer is legally allowed to pay.

A sculpture of Karl Marx

MIXED ECONOMY
An economy with a mix of privately owned industry and government planning and intervention.

MONEY
A medium of exchange; an item generally accepted as payment.

MONOPOLY
A company that has sole control over the sale of a good or service.

MORTGAGE
A type of loan, often used for house purchases. The lender legally owns the asset purchased with the borrowed money until the loan has been repaid.

NATIONALIZATION
The compulsory purchase or takeover of privately owned businesses by the government.

NATURAL RESOURCES
Materials and energy that occur naturally on Earth and have economic use and value, such as water, lumber, wind, and oil.

OUTPUT
The quantity of a good or service that is produced in a specific time.

PENSION
A regular payment to a retired person by a government or company.

POPULATION
The total number of people who inhabit an area or nation.

PRICE
The amount of money needed to purchase a particular good or service.

PRODUCTION
The process of making something.

PRODUCTIVITY
The rate at which something is produced per unit of input—for example, one hour of work.

PROFIT
The sum of money that is left over after all the expenses involved in producing and selling something are deducted.

RATE OF RETURN
The money received in a period of time (usually one year) as a result of an investment, expressed as a percentage of the cost of that investment. For example, if a person buys a field for $1,000 and rents it to another person for $100 per year, the rate of return is 10 percent per year.

RECESSION
A period in which economic activity declines and GDP shrinks.

RESOURCES
Raw materials, tools, or labor used to produce goods and services.

REVENUE
The income that a business receives before deductions are made for expenses and tax.

President Hugo Chavez of Venezuela has nationalized major industries, such as electricity, oil, and steel

SAVING
Putting money aside for future use.

SOCIALISM
A political theory that argues for state ownership of industry in order to achieve social and economic equality.

SERVICES
One of the main sectors of the economy, it includes all jobs in which expertise or activities are provided to paying customers, such as guiding tourists and firefighting.

SHADOW ECONOMY
The part of an economy that operates outside the law, such as selling illegal drugs or fake goods. It is also known as the black market.

A wind farm converts wind, a natural resource, into energy

A 1948 poster celebrating Bulgarian socialism

SHAREHOLDER
Someone who owns one or more shares in a company.

SHARES
Certificates proving part-ownership of a company that can be bought and sold on a stock market.

SOLVENCY
The ability to pay debts.

SPECULATION
Betting on the future value of an asset.

STAGNATION
The condition of an economy when it is neither growing nor shrinking.

STOCK
The quantity of a product that a seller currently owns. This is also another word for a share.

STOCKBROKER
A person who buys and sells shares on behalf of clients.

STOCK EXCHANGE
A place in which company shares are bought and sold.

SUPPLY
The quantity of a good or service sellers are willing and able to provide to buyers at a particular price.

TARIFF
A tax on goods transported from one nation to another.

TAXES
Money raised by governments through compulsory charges based on income, purchases, and property ownership.

TRADE
The exchange of goods and services, often conducted through the medium of money.

TRADE UNION
An association of working people that aims to improve working conditions and wages.

TRANSACTION COSTS
The costs involved in buying, selling, or transferring ownership of something.

UNEMPLOYMENT
Being without work. The unemployment rate is the percentage of the population that is willing to work but unable to find employment.

Unemployed men waiting outside a soup kitchen during the Great Depression

WORLD BANK
An international organization that provides financial assistance to developing countries.

WORLD TRADE ORGANIZATION
An international organization that monitors and enforces rules governing world trade.

Find out more

PLACES TO VISIT

- **THE UNITED STATES MINT**
  Denver, CO, and Philadelphia, PA
  www.usmint.gov/mint_tours
  The US Mint offers tours at its Denver and Philadelphia locations. You can learn about the history of coin manufacturing and today's state-of-the-art technology.

- **MONEY MUSEUM**
  Colorado Springs, CO
  www.money.org
  The American Numismatic Association's Money Museum features rare coins and other exhibits about the history of money.

- **NEW YORK FINANCIAL DISTRICT**
  New York, NY
  Several companies offer tours of the Wall Street neighborhood, including OnBoard Tours (see www.newyorkpartyshuttle.com).

- **FEDERAL RESERVE BANKS**
  Various US locations
  www.federalreserve.gov/OTHERFRB.HTM
  The US Federal Reserve System maintains 12 regional banks and associated branches. Most of these offer tours by appointment, giving fascinating insights into the inner workings of the US financial system.

- **THE BUREAU OF ENGRAVING AND PRINTING**
  Washington, DC, and Fort Worth, TX
  www.moneyfactory.gov/locations
  Visit either of the BEP's two locations and see millions of dollars being printed. Tours reveal each stage of the printing process, from blank sheets of paper to finished bills.

- **CHRISTIE'S, NEW YORK**
  New York, NY
  www.christies.com
  Visitors to the US headquarters of one of the world's most famous auction houses can visit auctions free of charge. Christie's also has branches in 31 other countries.

USEFUL WEBSITES

- This award-winning site provides a very readable introduction to economics and economic concepts:
  www.socialstudiesforkids.com/subjects/economicsbasic.htm

- This site contains fascinating galleries of banknotes from around the world:
  www.banknotes.com

- Learn about US dollar bills and their history at the official website of the US Bureau of Engraving and Printing:
  www.moneyfactory.gov

- As well as the history of the US Mint, this fun site has lots of money-related games:
  www.usmint.gov/kids/

Index

Acknowledgments

Dorling Kindersley would like to thank:
Steve Setford for editorial assistance; Stephanie Pliakas for proofreading; Jackie Brind for the index; David Ekholm|Album, Sunita Gahir, Jo Little, Sue Nicholson, Jessamy Wood, and Bulent Yusuf for the clipart; Sue Nicholson and Jo Little for the wallchart; and Camilla Hallinan and Dawn Henderson for editorial advice.

The publishers would like to thank the following for their kind permission to reproduce their photographs:

(Key: a-above; b-below/bottom; c-center; l-left; r-right; t-top)

akg-images: 49tl; Alamy Images: Frank Chmura 9tl; Corbis Super RF 31b; Eagle Visions Photography/Craig Lovell 9cl; Mary Evans Picture Library 68br; Jason Friend 17tr; David Gowans 44tl (Plane); Peter Horree 15tr; KPZ Foto 21tr; Martyn Vickery 30cr; Courtesy of Apple. Apple and the Apple logo are trademarks of Apple Computer Inc., registered in the US and other countries: 4cla, 6tr; The Art Archive: Musée du Louvre, Paris/Dagli Orti 16cl; Dagli Orti 68c; Private Collection/Marc Charmet 71tl; Tate Gallery, London/Eileen Tweedy 36bl; The Bridgeman Art Library: Collection of the New-York Historical Society 2c, 32tr; Delaware Art Museum, Wilmington 38tl; Dreamtime Gallery, London 13br; Private Collection 67clb; The Trustees of the British Museum: 2cr, 20br; Corbis: Craig Aurness 19b; Richard Baker 41bl, 47tl; Bettmann 10tl, 46cr, 50cr, 53tr, 71c; Car Culture 31cla; Condé Nast Archive 42tl; Keith Dannemiller 33bc; C. Devan 33cr; DPA/Tim Brakemeier 11tl; Tom Owen Edmunds 45tl; EPA/David Coll Blanco 45c; EPA/Hotli Simanjuntak 11c; EPA/STR 51tr; EPA/Yonhap 39cr; Eurasia Press/Steven Vidler 22b, 42cr; Free Agents Limited/Dallas and John Heaton 11tr; Michael Freeman 44b; The Gallery Collection 34cl; Porter Gifford 40b; Godong/

Pascal Deloche 37tl; Klaus Hackenberg 27tr; Historical Picture Archive 23tc; Andrew Holbrooke 55cra; Angelo Hornak 30bl; Image Source 15bc; JAI/Gavin Hellier 51br; JAI/Walter Bibikow 10b; Wolfgang Kaehler 54bl; Bob Krist 42cl; Kim Kulish 31tr; Frans Lanting 31tc; Gideon Mendel 26b, 58-59bc; Hans Peter Merten 47tr; Jean Miele 35t; Gianni Dagli Orti 6cl, 66cl; PoodlesRock 66tr; Ryan Pyle 18br; Redlink 60cl; Reuters/Alexander Natruskin 48br; Reuters/Brendan McDermid 40tr; Reuters/Jagadeesh 53tl; Reuters/Jo Yong-Hak 51cl; Reuters/Marcos Brindicci 70cr; Reuters/Yuriko Nakao 27br; Gregor Schuster 26tr; David Selman 59cl; Star Ledger/Mark Dye 52-53b; Rudy Sulgan 69br; Sygma/Paulo Fridman 56-57c; Murat Taner 6-7b; William Taufic 7tl; Liba Taylor 45tr; TWPhoto 53cl; Visions of America/Joseph Sohm 42bl, 48cl, 70-71b; Mark Weiss 21tl; Westend 61/Fotofeeling 43tl; Xinhua Press/Lui Lei 31c; Zefa/Matthias Kulka 29c; Zefa/Ursula Klawitter 62bc; Dorling Kindersley: Courtesy of The American Museum of Natural History/Lynton Gardiner 2tl, 13c; The British Museum, London/Chas Howson 20bc, 20tr, 21br; The British Museum, London/Tina Chambers 66cb; Confederate Memorial Hall, New Orleans/Dave King 46c (Hat); Courtesy of the Gettysburg National Military Park, PA/Dave King 46cb (Gun); Judith Miller/Huxtins 39tl; Courtesy of The Museum of London 46tl, 12tl (Bark & Berries); Courtesy of the Pitt Rivers Museum, University of Oxford/Dave King 20cb; Courtesy of the Royal Geographical Society, London 32tl; Courtesy of the US Army Heritage and Education Center - Military History Institute/Dave King 46clb (Jacket); Getty Images: AFP/Ahmad Al-Rubaye 8cl, 63tr; AFP/Alexander Joe 49b; AFP/Dominique Faget 41br; AFP/Fabrice Coffrini 55tc; AFP/Hoang Dinh Nam 33tr; AFP/Issouf Sanogo 54cl; AFP/Jeff Haynes 35cr; AFP/Jimin Lai 37tr; AFP/Jung Yeon-Je 28-29bc; AFP/Michael Latz 32b; AFP/Roberto Schmidt 19tr; AFP/Roslan Rahman 29br; AFP/Shah Marai 29tr; AFP/Torsten Blackwood 9br; AFP/Uwe Meinhold 70tc; Asia Images/Marcus Mok 5, 27cla; Asia Images/Rex Butcher 25b; Blend

Images/Stewart and Pam Ostrow 61crb; Blue Jean Images 9cra; The Bridgeman Art Library 18crb, 18tr, 24bl; Paula Bronstein 63cr; China Photos 14bl; Digital Vision/Jorg Greuel 65cr; Digital Vision/Lauren Nicole 4br, 61tr; Evening Standard 49tr; FPG/Hulton Archive 38-39b; Christopher Furlong 23cr, 57tr; Gallo Images/Andrew Bannister 12-13bc; Glowimages 61l; Hulton Archive 17b; Iconica/Grant V. Faint 18clb; The Image Bank/Barros & Barros 57br; The Image Bank/Mitchell Kanashkevich 45cr; Mike Kemp 62cl; Alex Livesey 37b; Lonely Planet Images/Jane Sweeney 24tl; Peter Macdiarmid 41cr; National Geographic/Richard Nowitz 4crb, 29tl; PhotoAlto Agency/Isabelle Rozenbaum and Frederic Cirou 69tl; Photodisc/Peter Adams 13tr; Photographer's Choice/Andrew Paterson 1, 27tl; Photographer's Choice/Ariel Skelley 41tl; Photographer's Choice/Burazin 44tl (Background); Photographer's Choice/C Squared Studios 59t; Photographer's Choice/Fabian Gonzales 11bc; Photographer's Choice/Frank Lukasseck 60-61c; Photographer's Choice/Gavin Hellier 62-63c; Photographer's Choice/Gregor Schuster 23br; Photographer's Choice/John Lamb 8r; Photographer's Choice/Nacivet 7tr; Photographer's Choice/Sam Armstrong 46l; Photographer's Choice/Still Images 58l; Photographer's Choice/Tim Hawley 65b; Photonica/Phillip Simpson 8bl; Photonica/Steven Puetzer 68tc; Steven Puetzer 3c, 34-35b; Riser/Barry Wong 22tl; Sebun Photo/R. Creation 43b; StockFood Creative 59cr; Stone/Frans Lemmens 47b; Stone/James Worrell 47cr; Stone/Joseph Van Os 59br; Stone/Peter Adams 4bl, 23tl; Taxi/Vikki Hart 26tl; Time Life Pictures/Victor Englebert 13tl; Topical Press Agency 52cl; Ian Waldie 61cra; from Adam Smith An Inquiry into the Nature and Causes of the Wealth of Nations, 1764: 16crb; Govind Mittal 17clb; iStockphoto.com: 2bl, 2bl (Jerry Can), 19tl, 21cl, 48tr (Jerry Can); Pawel Bartkowski 63br; Dawn Liljenquist 16crb; Max Popov 2ca, 23ca; Ivan Stevanovic 56cl; Library Of Congress, Washington, DC: 35cl, 50cl; Martin Wilson: 52tl; Museum of the National Bank of Belgium, Brussels: 24cl; Panos Pictures:

G.M.B. Akash 58clb; Photolibrary: AGE Fotostock/Jose Fuste Raga 30cl; AGE Fotostock/Morales 14r; Photononstop/Nicholas Thibaut 23tr; Press Association Images: AP Photo/Karel Navarro 15clb; Department of Justice 51tl; Rex Features: 50-51bc; Richard Gardner 15.1clb; SanDisk Corporation: 55cblc; Scripophily.com - The Gift of History: 34tr; Shutterstock: 64-65 (Background), 66-67 (Background), 68-69 (Background), 70-71 (Background); Still Pictures: Joerg Boethling 54-55c; Transit/Christiane Eisler 7cr.

Wallchart: Alamy Images: Corbis Super RF (Boardroom Meeting); Corbis: Bettmann (Adam Smith), (Karl Marx); Eurasia Press/Steven Vidler (Market); Gideon Mendel (Industrial Robots); Reuters/Jagadeesh (Call Center); David Selman (Coffee Beans); Murat Taner (Container Ships); Dorling Kindersley: The British Museum, London/Chas Howson (Lydian Coins); Courtesy of the Museum of London (Hunter Gatherers Bark & Berries); Getty Images: Asia Images/Rex Butcher (Hong Kong Banking); Blend Images/Stewart Cohen and Pam Ostrow (Wheelchair Man); Digital Vision/Lauren Nicole (Petrol Pump); FPG/Hulton Archive (Great Depression); Photodisc/Steven Puetzer (Bull & Bear); Stone/James Worrell (Diamond Rings); iStockphoto.com: (Debit Cards); Photolibrary: Photononstop/Nicholas Thibaut (Camel Traders).

All other images © Dorling Kindersley
For further information see: www.dkimages.com